The Meaning of Music

A STUDY IN PSYCHOLOGICAL AESTHETICS

By Carroll C. Pratt

Professor of Psychology Emeritus
Princeton University
Chairman and Professor of Psychology
Rider College

With a New Introduction

JOHNSON REPRINT CORPORATION

New York and London

1968

INTRODUCTION

The main thesis of this book, when it first appeared some thirty-five years ago, was that the enduring qualities of music are *presented* in the tonal structure itself. They are not associations, emotions, reveries, moods, or any other attributes contributed by the listener. Music is stimulus-bound. To call music sad or gay is not a pathetic fallacy, for tonal perception along with every other kind of perception is replete with qualities that can only be described—and then all too inadequately— by the use of words that apply to human moods: pensive, fervent, tranquil, somber, agitated, languid, pompous, and the like.

On rereading the book I became aware that this view of perception, and of music, had not stood out as prominently as I could now wish, partly because at that time perception was still dealt with largely in the classical tradition. Perception was the analysis of space, distance, time, size, localization, direction, movement, and other factors, in the various sense modalities, not the immediate and direct awareness of the hospitality of a greeting, the friendliness of a gesture, the sprightly and cheerful expression on a child's face, the monotony of a voice, the drabness of a room, the mysterious fascination of Leonardo's paintings, or the quiet melancholy of some of Mozart's music. So in this Introduction I should like to clarify, if possible, and make more explicit a view of perception that in recent years has aroused wide interest in psychology and made important contributions to aesthetics.[1]

[1] This view of perception has been developed and elaborately

The main argument of the book is concerned chiefly with music. The theme of the argument, however, can with only slight variation be transposed to other arts, with the possible exception of those that use words as the medium of communication. The material of drama, poetry, and literature is symbolic in the sense that the first term—the sight or sound of words—is effective largely to the extent to which it subexcites memories and ideas which transcend the sensuous medium of the verbal material itself. The form of poetry, drama, and literature may be important, and important perhaps in that order; but if the extra-formal properties of these arts were left out of account, the material of some of them would hardly have more appeal than the Ebbinghaus nonsense syllables of the psychological laboratory. In architecture, in sculpture, and especially |in painting, on the other hand, the importance of form has never been denied. Yet in these arts too the *meaning* of the form adds to appreciation an element which depends more upon the individual who loves the object than upon the properties of the object itself. Only in music is the meaning of the form identical with the form itself. Here content and form are one—whatever that phrase means.

The finest music of the great German classicists—

expounded for the most part by the Gestalt psychologists, Max Wertheimer, Kurt Koffka, and Wolfgang Köhler. Its newest and most effective exposition may be found in the writings of J. J. Gibson, especially in his *The Perception of the Visual World* (Houghton Mifflin, 1950) and *The Senses Considered as Perceptual Systems* (Houghton Mifflin, 1966).

Bach, Handel, Haydn, Mozart, Beethoven, Schubert, and even Brahms and Bruckner—lends itself especially well to the study and evaluation of pure form. The quartets, quintets, sonatas, and symphonies of those composers have no meaning in the usual sense of that word. Their glory is in the power of sound, not in the representation of objects nor in the expression of ideas. Music aesthetics is shot through with confusion and debate, except on one point. Almost everyone agrees that music in and of itself—absolute music, as it is sometimes called—is not an adequate medium for the communication of thoughts or the delineation of objects. In the narrow domain of onomatopoeia, to be sure, a clever arrangement of notes may serve as an iconic symbol. But even in the cantatas of Bach or the oratorios of Haydn the device is used sparingly. At best it may help to reinforce a mood which could be expressed just as well without imitative props. At worst the device is merely the occasion for a smile.

Music presents mood and feeling, not external fact and logical discourse. Schubert can tell us that his heart with pleasure fills, but he must leave to Wordsworth, or else to sheer guess, the specification of the cause. Therein lies the big difference between music and all the other arts. The latter also may express mood and feeling, but always indirectly by way of symbols, unless their form is deliberately stripped of all meaning, a goal which some contemporary painting seems to have achieved with a goodly measure of success. In music the presentation of mood is direct, for the way in which the tonal material is put together by the composer constitutes the very essence of auditory mood, the gaiety or the melancholy of the music itself.

Music at its best is not symbolic at all. The theory, or rather, the topic of symbolism as dealt with by modern philosophy has become so mazy and tortuous that the only way to rediscover what "symbolism" or "symbol" means is to look the words up in a dictionary. Webster defines "symbol" as "that which suggests something else by reason of association, especially, a visible sign of something invisible"; and "symbolism" he defines as "artistic imitation or invention, not as an end in itself but as a method of suggesting immaterial, ideal, or otherwise intangible truth or states." In contrast to these definitions, the thesis of this book is that tonal form stands for nothing beyond itself. It does not suggest mood and feeling. It *is* mood and feeling. The qualities of auditory perception are not iconic signs, nor do they by themselves represent or imitate or copy anything. In conjunction with words and action they may of course acquire all sorts of heteronymous meanings; but such meanings, however enjoyable they may be to dreamy-eared listeners, are not tonal stuff nor do they necessarily have anything to do with the intrinsic quality of tonal design. Tonal form represents only itself. The form and content of music are one.

An attempt will be made presently to find an appropriate and proper interpretation of phrases which imply that form and content are one, that music is an end in itself. At first such phrases sound like acknowledgments

of defeat uttered by an exhausted formalist, words
running in circles, signifying nothing. If rightly understood, however, they furnish a clue to the only music
aesthetics which makes sense and which at the same
time also does justice to the marvels of tonal art. They
assert boldly and dogmatically that music is not a
language, even if they do not indicate too clearly what
else it may be. A language is a system of symbols, a
device to carry the mind by way of association beyond
the thing presented into a different universe of discourse. Language is a means to an end, not an end in
itself. A symbol can be an end in itself only if it serves
no other purpose—a state of affairs which by definition
is a contradiction in terms.

It is indeed true that music, more than any other art,
has often been called, ever since the beginnings of
aesthetic and critical speculation, the language of emotion. "Music stands quite alone," said Schopenhauer.
"It is cut off from all the other arts. It does not express
a particular and definite joy, sorrow, anguish, delight,
or mood of peace, but joy, sorrow, anguish, delight,
peace of mind *themselves,* in the abstract, in their
essential nature, without accessories, and therefore
without their customary motives. Yet it enables us to
grasp and share them in their full quintessence." No
serious objection need be raised to calling music the
language of emotion, provided one bears in mind that
music is neither a language nor an emotion. In every
other respect the phrase is all right, even valuable and
provocative; for it raises a question which it is the

business of aesthetics to answer. How does it happen
that to speak of music as the language of emotion seems
to strike the nail so squarely on the head?

Art in general and music in particular have been
said to embody emotion, to make objective the subjective life of mankind. If these and similar expressive
phrases are taken as mere figures of speech, they may
be accepted for what they are worth—which is not
much. Aesthetics is not a science, whatever else it may
be; and writers in the field should perhaps be allowed
the same poetic license which is granted to the artist
himself. To say that music embodies emotion, however,
is to assert the impossible, if the phrase is taken literally.
The material of emotion is bodily process, an elaborate
pattern of muscular and visceral disturbance. An emotion has its location and existence literally inside the
corporeal structure of the person who is in possession
of the experience. In spite of the objections which have
been raised to certain aspects of the famous James-
Lange theory of emotion, no critic has ever denied the
validity of the theory with respect to its insistence upon
organic, kinesthetic, cutaneous, muscular, and visceral
sensation as the *sine qua non* of emotion. Without these
sensations there can be no emotion. The material of
music, on the other hand, is in no part compounded of
these sensations, from which it obviously must follow
that music within itself contains no emotion, nor does
it embody or objectify any experience that can be
rightly called by that name. Music is tonal, emotion is
visceral—two quite different areas of sensory discourse.

To say that music embodies emotion is therefore either to utter nonsense or to speak in metaphor, which in neither case throws any light on the question at issue.

The whole problem would be neatly and quickly solved if it could be shown that music arouses real emotion in the listener; if it could be demonstrated that the poignant grief of the last movement of the Tchaikovsky *Sixth*, for example, had its origin in the visceral commotion of the audience rather than in the design of the tonal structure. Unfortunately the evidence for this view is limited to a relatively small and perhaps unimportant segment of the audience. The view is therefore not exactly wrong. It is indeed perhaps right as far as it goes. The only trouble is that it goes hardly far enough to get up off the ground. A few people do undoubtedly soak in some sort of emotional bath while listening to the heart-rending measures of Tchaikovsky or to the sickening despair of Ravel; but for every one whose visceral processes are thus aroused there are ninety and nine who in proper psychical distance gladly lend an attentive ear to the sadness of Tchaikovsky and the sorrow of Ravel without themselves descending into any slough of despond. If to hear the intense grief of the fugal passages of the *Eroica* required real tears and adrenal secretions, then an anomalous if not impossible psychological state would have to prevail. The gorgeous clash of dissonant minor seconds which brings the tremendous but short fugue to an incomplete close— several measures of almost unbearable anguish—has been a source of supreme delight to countless lovers of music. How can a listener be at once pleased and pained? The answer must be that something is wrong with a theory which makes such impossible and contradictory demands upon human nature. If the lover of music finds delight in the melancholy of Mozart and the sadness of Beethoven, these qualities must somehow be closely bound up with the music itself, for visceral sorrow and sighing can hardly proceed from the listener who is at the same time filled with pleasure.

One further drawback should in passing be noted in connection with any theory of emotional arousal. Presumably according to such views the excellence of a work of art must be in some way related to the intensity of emotional involvement. This criterion would degrade all works of art to an estate far below many everyday events which have no claim whatever to artistic merit. Loss at poker, death of a friend, unrequited love, success or failure in business or professional pursuits: these and countless similar mundane accidents raise havoc in a realm of adrenal action which the artist could never hope nor ever want to penetrate.

The most widely accepted theory with respect to the place or presence of emotion in art is probably that of *Einfühlung*. The doctrine of empathy, as originally expounded by Theodor Lipps around 1900, was an attempt to account for the many qualities in visual and auditory perception which appeared inexplicable in terms of the sensory dimensions of the classical psychology of that period. In vision, for example, the accepted attributes were hue, tint, saturation, protensity, intensity, and extensity. If the problem under investigation happened to be, let us say, the relation between the brightness of the total field and a patch of color in the foveal area, these attributes were effective instruments for analysis and generalization. But what about the many qualities which laymen and artists alike constantly ascribe to things which they see: the gracefulness of lines, the sharp angularity of shapes, the depressing heaviness of certain styles of architecture, to say nothing of the gloom of wet winter afternoons, the gaiety of spring mornings, and the cheerful smile of a sprightly child? Where do such qualities come from? Are they properties which belong to the visual field? Classical psychology either ignored the problem or turned it over to the theory of associationism, or to its first cousin, the doctrine of empathy. Both of these explanatory principles were as one in the assertion that the ascription of sprightliness or gloom to things seen or heard is a pathetic fallacy, permissible perhaps to poets, but not to men in possession of their wits, and certainly not to art critics and never to professors of aesthetics.

The gracefulness or awkwardness of a line, said Lipps and his followers, is not, strictly speaking, a property of the line at all. The visualness of a line is protensity, plus extensity, plus a given intensity of figure in relation to that of ground. If the line is called graceful it is because the movement of the eyes in surveying it is smooth and easy-flowing, in contrast to the jerky and jumpy eye movements produced by a so-called awkward line. It is the smoothness or jerkiness of ocular kinesthesis which lends to visual experience the quality of gracefulness or awkwardness. The almost inescapable connection between the feel of the muscles and the look of the line is part of the magic of empathy. It is the line itself which seems to be graceful or awkward, although in actual point of fact these qualities have their origin in another sense modality, in the low and unaesthetic region of muscle action.

It was not until careful and accurate photographs of eye movements were made that serious doubt was first cast upon the doctrine of empathy. These photographs furnished irrefutable evidence that the eyes in scanning the visual field move more or less in the same way, regardless of the content of the field. Eye movements involved in running over a graceful line are no different from those set into operation by an awkward line. In both cases, as in reading and in almost every kind of ocular activity, the movements constitute a series of stops and starts. If therefore the qualities of the lines are not determined and differentiated by the eye movements, it would seem to follow that they are intrinsic aspects of the visual material itself. By the same token it may be assumed that the qualities of tonal form—the sadness of a melody, the lilt of a rhythm, the solemnity of full harmonies in slow chordal progression—have their origin in auditory perception rather than in the accretions and projections of kinesthetic sensation. In trying to account for these ever-present and over-all characteristics of sight and sound it is not only unnecessary to appeal to the doctrine of empathy, it would seem to be in most instances actually wrong.

In the areas of visual and auditory perception that are involved in the appreciation of fine art, the doctrine of empathy raises more serious and baffling problems than it solves, if indeed it can be said to solve any problems at all. The doctrine implies that what the lover of art discovers in his objects of admiration are qualities which in the last analysis are projections of his own inner self, just as at the level of the simpler perceptions the awkwardness, let us say, of a line is said to be the ascription to the visual field of the jerkiness of eye movements. The skillful rhythmic patterns and rapturous movements of ballet, the dazzling tonal fireworks of full orchestra or the quiet serenity of muted strings, the moving radiance of ever-changing color in the windows of Chartres, the sweetness and sadness and tenderness of Renaissance madonnas, the powerful soaring of Gothic columns and vaults: these and countless other art forms derive their chief glory not from the artists who produce them, but rather from the people who look at them and listen to them.

It was not Bach who injected such power and majesty into his fugues, nor Beethoven who found the means of expressing unearthly tranquility in some of the movements of his later quartets, nor was it Mozart who wove melancholy and disillusion into the elegant texture of his quintets. It is you and I who perform these miracles. It is we who are responsible for the long heavenly charm of Schubert's symphonies and for the

romantic *Sturm und Drang* in Brahms' trios. It is for us
to blush, not for Wagner to be ashamed, when the
indecent exposures of the *Liebestod* sound forth from
the stage and orchestra pit. Tonal design cannot be
erotic, nor serene, nor majestic. These qualities have
their origin in the viscera of the listener, and are projected by him into the auditory perceptions. The composer is not an artist. He is a trained technician, at times
an amazing magician, who cleverly manipulates pitch
and rhythm. After he has put his notes together, all he
can do is to sit back and wait until the artistic geniuses
in the audience create out of his tonal design the
masterpieces which in his innocence or vanity he probably assumed he himself had contrived. The doctrine of
empathy is not ordinarily stated in exactly this way,
but if I am not gravely mistaken, the implications of
the doctrine are precisely those just cited. And by
these implications the doctrine falls.

Other views have been proposed for the purpose of
explaining the manner in which emotion finds expression in art, and especially in music. None of them,
however, is satisfactory, for they share in common with
the views already described the conviction that real
emotion is present in the musical experience. This
conviction is the source of most of the difficulty.

The whole problem might be solved if the inconvenient and stubborn business of emotion could be
gotten rid of; if, in other words, the disagreeable and
unwanted baby could be poured out with the bath
water. Well, it is just that action which is contemplated

in the present treatment of the problem, not for the purpose of ignoring or avoiding the difficulty, but rather because the facts dictate just that action. The troublesome baby—i.e., emotion in music—turns out to be an illusion. With a clear and easy conscience one may therefore watch the mirage go down the drain.

The Gordian knot is cut, as it were, by full recognition of the fact that real emotion, although it may be aroused in a few listeners, is neither a necessary nor a sufficient condition, nor indeed any kind of condition, for the creation and existence of the expressive qualities of tonal form. By expressive qualities I mean those characteristics of music which are so quickly and accurately identified by the average listener, but so inadequately described by such adjectives as exhilarating, martial, somber, yearning, pensive, erotic, agitated, languid—those qualities without which music would not be music, the extreme formalists like Hanslick to the contrary notwithstanding. Let these qualities be called the *tertiary qualities* of music, a term which has of late appeared rather frequently in aesthetics to designate expressive form.

It is to the great credit of *Gestalttheorie* that it has sensitized psychologists to the existence and importance of tertiary qualities in perception and at the same time to the sorry plight of these qualities in modern theory. The position taken in the present argument follows closely that of *Gestalttheorie*. The point of view hardly needs specific recapitulation, for it has been implied throughout the preceding critique of emotion in art, and can perhaps best be expounded by trying to make clear why the position has not been made manifest and accepted long before now.

Modern experimental psychology, the psychology of the laboratory, sometimes referred to today as classical psychology, had its beginnings in Germany during the middle and latter part of the last century. In an effort to make a place for itself in the hierarchy of sciences it followed feverishly the practice of the older sciences of searching for basic elements, of ferreting out in this case the elements of experience, the dimensions of consciousness. Unfortunately these elements or dimensions shortly became the sole objects of investigation without regard to the tertiary qualities in which they were originally embedded. Hue, tint, pitch, timbre, volume, extensity, intensity: these attributes of sensation became the subject matter of classical psychology. If the gracefulness or exhilaration or agitation of perceptual experience ever came in for consideration, it was turned over to Theodor Lipps and his followers. Such qualities were not in the visual or auditory modalities. They were empathic projections from the domain of muscle and viscera. The theory of empathy relieved classical psychology of all responsibility with respect to tertiary qualities.

A far more important reason for the neglect of tertiary qualities in perception and art has been the confusion ever since the beginnings of philosophical speculation about the nature and location of emotion. The confusion indeed goes far beyond the boundaries of philosophy and psychology, for it permeates the very language which everyone speaks. The words which are used to describe emotion are also drawn upon to denote experiences which are not emotions at all. The psychological occasion which has everywhere brought about the use of the same words for two different kinds of experience lies also at the root of much of the confounding of aesthetic theory.

Let us consider one example. The word "agitated" refers in many instances to a bodily commotion which clearly belongs within the realm of emotion. The experience is difficult to describe in spite of its ease of recognition. It involves jumpy sensations, inability to keep still, restlessness, tension, an over-all muscular and visceral disturbance which is unquestionably located literally inside the person who reports the experience. It is a form or pattern which is compounded of bodily processes. Yet the same form or pattern—and here we arrive at the core of the argument—the same pattern can be compounded of processes which are not bodily nor internal at all, which have their origin in the visual or auditory modalities. We say that the waves of the sea appear agitated, that in storm or wind the sounds of the forest are agitated, or for our purposes still better, that a passage of music is agitated. In these instances the pattern or form described as agitated is composed of material which is completely outside the realm of emotion. Yet in aesthetic theory it has been taken for granted that if a passage of music is described as agitated, or tranquil, or wistful, these qualities must in some way embody genuine emotion, or at least, empathic projection. The mistake is quite natural and understandable, but it is nevertheless a mistake.

Similar examples could be given in the case of all words used to describe mood and feeling. The same words apply equally well to qualities in visual and auditory perceptions. A person may feel in a somber mood, but it is likewise true that certain combinations or patterns of color or sound are fittingly described as somber. A lilting rhythm may be visual or auditory or organic. If the rhythm is organic, chances are the person will say that he himself feels in a lilting mood, whereas the same rhythm in the other sense departments presents itself to the eye and ear without any bodily commotion, and therefore without emotion.

A simple illustration of similarity of form between two different sense departments has been made familiar in the literature of *Gestalttheorie*. Figure 1 illustrates two meaningless forms. The reader will be able to decide without any trouble which of the meaningless sounds, *uloomu* and *takete*, applies to which form. The illustration shows that impressions from different sense departments may be very similar with respect to form. Each of the sounds, *takete* and *uloomu*, fits perfectly one of the visual designs, but not the other.

The ease and accuracy with which listeners can identify the moods, i.e., the tertiary qualities, of music can be shown by asking them to match passages of music to adjectives that are intended to describe the moods. The following example is chosen from many

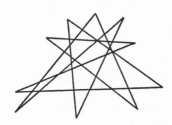

FIG. 1

such procedures that I have used over the years. A group of 227 college students was given the task of assigning adjectives, by the method of matching, to four recorded passages of music: the introductory measures of Brahm's *First Symphony,* about forty measures in the middle cf Mendelssohn's overture to *A Midsummer Night's Dream,* the transitional passage between the third and fourth movements of Mozart's string *Quintet in G-minor,* and several measures from the third movement of Tchaikovsky's *Sixth Symphony.* Experts in a department of music had agreed that the passage from Brahms could best be described as *stately,* the measures from Mendelssohn as *sprightly,* the transitional movement from Mozart as *wistful,* and the measures from Tchaikovsky as *vigorous.* These four adjectives were written on the blackboard in alphabetical order, and the students were told to assign to each composition the adjective they considered most appropriate. The compositions were played through twice in random order. If the students made their judgments by sheer chance, they would have been about 25 percent correct. If the judgments exceeded 25 percent by an appreciable margin, it would appear that something in the music was coercive or compelling in leading the students to select one adjective rather than another. The high uniformity in the results has been characteristic of these procedures, both in music and in judging the moods of abstract visual designs. In this instance all of the compositions were judged more than 90 percent "correct" by the students, as can be seen in Table I.

TABLE I

PERCENTAGE OF CASES, IN ROUND NUMBERS, IN WHICH THE ADJECTIVES IN THE HORIZONTAL COLUMN WERE JUDGED APPROPRIATE TO COMPOSITIONS LISTED IN THE VERTICAL COLUMN

	Stately	Sprightly	Wistful	Vigorous
Brahms	92	0	3	5
Mendelssohn	0	99	0	1
Mozart	3	0	97	0
Tchaikovsky	6	2	0	92

None of the theories designed to account for music as a language of emotion makes it clear how these results can be explained. The compositions can not be said to *embody* emotion. That view is definitely ruled out. Nor is it reasonable to assume that real emotions were aroused in the listeners. The students looked somewhat bored by the experiment, or at best mildly amused. The theory of empathy also makes it necessary to assume that the students had at least incipient subjective moods which by a process of projection led to the selection of the proper adjective, a possibility which is again hardly likely. Did these young men have a feeling of stateliness within them while they were listening to Brahms? They certainly did not look sprightly during the playing of Mendelssohn. Did Mozart make them feel wistful? A few of them may have felt a bit wistful, and then experienced a quick shift to a more vigorous internal state when the full orchestra and the big chords of Tchaikovsky came at them. It is of course conceivable that the students were ascribing their own emotional states to the music. The method gives no guarantee against such a pathetic fallacy. It strains credulity, however, to believe that such a large group of undergraduates would experience such homogeneity of feeling at precisely the right moments. No. These young people were not reporting their own sprightly feelings, their wistful moods, or their stately affections. They were selecting from the list presented them those words which best described the auditory structures of the music to which they were listening.

Music used in such experiments is usually written in a familiar idiom of Western culture, and although few of the subjects in the above experiment actually were able to name the pieces they had heard, the objection can be made that they knew the kind of verbal labels scholars and critics have attached to the passages chosen. In order to examine this objection, a student of mine did a matching experiment in which cacophonous and unfamliar selections by more recent composers (Hindemith, Berg, Stravinsky, and Bartok) were listened to by 113 subjects. The "correct" matchings ranged from 70 percent to 97 percent, a bit lower than for familiar music, but all of them way above chance. Music is a complex perception. Styles may change, but the ear apparently can detect in their varieties certain groupings of tones that are coercive in presenting the tertiary qualities of mood.

Opinion is widespread that cultural factors play a decisive role in aesthetic preference. Yet there is some evidence that this opinion is in need of revision. Feelings and moods must be pretty much the same the world over. If so, then their expression in outward form would presumably have elements in common across cultures, however much obscured at first by stereotypes and peculiarities of time and place. Another student of mine managed to find a musicologist who had studied the moods represented by Bedouin, Indonesian, Javanese, Korean, and Maori folk music. Ten typical examples and ten adjectives chosen by the expert were presented in random order to 73 undergraduates for matching. The outlandish sounds caused both laughter and aversion, yet the "correct" matchings ranged from 77 percent to a high of 99 percent for a Bedouin piece of music that was supposed to have something to do with love. Studies of this kind are still too few to permit of any weighty conclusion, but they suggest that cultural relativism has gone a bit too far.[2]

A serious difficulty in cross-cultural studies is bound up with the very nature of tonal structure, or rather, with the manner in which the ear apprehends tonal designs of any complexity. The ear is a selective instrument. What is "out there" as far as the sounds themselves are concerned is often selectively rearranged in such a way as to obscure certain parts and favor others. If the reader wants a striking illustration of the selective nature of the ear, let him play over to himself or to friends the music printed in Fig. 2. The task is not to identify the mood of the music, but rather, what should be much simpler, to pick out a well-known melody concealed somewhere within the tonal design. It can be said with almost complete assurance that nearly everyone in this country has heard the melody again and again. No note has been altered. What is the melody?

The notes of the melody have been surrounded by different harmonies from those one is accustomed to hear and are embedded in the minor rather than the customary major mode. This alteration in tonal context produces such a novel effect that even the trained musician usually finds it impossible at first to hear the well-known sequence of notes.[3] So it might be with the members of any group, unaccustomed to Western or

[2] For a critical review of some of the studies in this field see my article, "Aesthetics," *Annual Review of Psychology,* 1961, 12, 71–93.

Fig. 2

Oriental music, if they were asked to identify the mood of what they heard. Failure would not prove that the mood was not there. The tertiary qualities, i.e., the tonal moods of auditory structure, are inherent in the music, not projected or read into it by the listener. It might simply mean that some momentarily more salient characteristic of the music obscured the mood.

It goes without saying, of course, that in listening to music for pleasure the moods are as a rule not recognized, let alone given a name, *Gott sei Dank*. In this book they are dealt with as somewhat artificial abstractions—although no less real on that account—for purposes of psychological study in an effort to find out

[3] I once played the passage to a friend who knew nothing about music and even liked to boast that he was tone-deaf. When I had finished he said, "That sounds to me like . . . ." and to my astonishment he named the melody correctly.

what it is in music that has such a tenacious hold on
many people.

Music perhaps more than any other art is filled with
tertiary qualities which duplicate very closely the
tertiary qualities of muscle and viscera. Music sounds
as though it were saturated with mood and feeling, and
for that reason has for centuries been called the language of emotion. But music speaks of emotion only
by way of tonal patterns which at the level of form are
indistinguishable from the patterns of bodily reverbera-
tions. *Music sounds the way emotions feel.*

Aesthetic form may be taken to mean the way in
which the parts of any work of art go together. Balance,
rhythm, harmony, line, contour, unity in variety, recapitulation, cadence, consonance, inversion, variation,
perspective: these and other similar factors are the
commodities which in the writings of many philosophers and in the shop talk of most artists seem to
constitute the very essence of art. It is quite right that
their importance should not be underestimated, especially in music. Music as a kaleidoscope of ever-changing tonal configuration has been a source of wondrous
delight all the way from two-part inventions to the art
of fugue. The extraordinary skill of most composers in
this respect, with the great Bach at their head, has given
strong support to formalists like Hanslick. Yet it is the
main contention of this book that musical form has
another property, far more important than any arrangement of parts; a quality without which tonal form
would hardly be music at all.

The most salient properties of form are tertiary qualities. These qualities are neither accretions nor associations acquired by the action of symbolic reference.
They are intrinsic properties of finely conceived tonal
design. A fugue as an exercise in tonal construction can
be composed tolerably well by second-rate students in
every conservatory of music, but hardly once in a century does such a fugue reveal anything like the mag-
nificent qualities of the G-Minor, or the St. Anne, or
the B-Minor—fugues with such majestic design, relentless predestination of plan, and lofty elevation of mood
that many worshippers of music have come to believe
that B-A-C-H is the proper spelling of God.

There is still another aspect of art which may well
be the most important of all, but which for lack of
competence I shall deal with only briefly in these concluding paragraphs. All art fulfills a human need. No
human activity above the level of the biological necessities is everywhere so widespread and tenacious as the
creation of objects of art, from which it must follow
that art *does* something which is important and useful.
Aesthetic theory which stops short with analysis of form
fails to take into account the function of art. Form is
what a work of art *is*. Function is what a work of art
does.

What then is the function or purpose of music? What
does music do? Inquiry into this phase of art and music
is a much more recent development as compared with
the time-honored interest in form. An explanation of
why it is that art does what it apparently does to people

will eventually turn into a statement of *what* happens
and *how*, for in the last analysis science never has any
answer to *why* which can go beyond the enumeration
of what conditions underlie the event under consideration. But aesthetics is a long way from the last analysis,
so in the meantime attempts at explanation are valuable.

It is obvious that the function of art is somehow
bound up with the deepest cravings and needs of mankind, otherwise art would have died out long ago, if
indeed it would ever have been born. The study of
human need and craving is still in its infancy, certainly
a long way from explanations which can be converted
into fact. The guesses in this area, the theories of personality, are therefore profitable and provocative, and
their extension into the field of aesthetics has already
given significant hints regarding the utility and function of art.

The function of art, according to these newer views
of personality, is to release from inner bondage the
energy of suppressed desire. The seed for the development of this idea in the field of aesthetics was contained
in Freud's theory of wit. The explosion of laughter,
thought Freud, can be accounted for by the deception
practiced upon the social censor by double meanings.
The socially acceptable meaning conceals within it a
forbidden thought. The latter, under the protection of
the former, slips through the mask of personality. The
unexpected release of a forbidden idea is an intensely
pleasant surprise. The result is a laugh.

The preoccupation of Freud with sex made his writings at first socially unacceptable, and from the point of view of psychophysiology too narrowly confined. Yet his analysis of personality unquestionably reveals the needle-witted penetration of genius. Release of a repressed impulse by means of a parlor-car joke may cause laughter in certain quarters, but the contrivance differs only in degree from the profound satisfaction which almost all mortals derive from the contemplation of any performance or object which makes manifest the latent content of the human spirit. In art the sudden glory of laughter is softened and prolonged and the memory of it is a joy forever, whereas the joke of yesterday is already stale and tomorrow it will be gone beyond recall.

The mental activity of all people, except perhaps that of the lowest specimens, is from childhood until old age in excess of the amount of actual muscular activity which is required for dealing with the external environment. Only a small fraction of human thought is ever translated into action. In the central region of the nervous system there flourishes during the lifetime of every individual an incessant cerebration which can neither be acted upon nor adequately expressed. In infancy every member of the human species runs head on into innumerable variations of the prohibition, "Thou shalt not." A good deal of what was intended by biological nature has been by human, nature forbidden. Two worlds thus come into existence and into various degrees of conflict, the inner world of desire and hope and the outer world of accomplishment. The degree to which desire exceeds accomplishment is a measure of the world of fantasy and imagination, and that measure for most sensitive and intelligent people is very large indeed.

It has come as something of a surprise, if not a shock, to learn how elaborate even in childhood are the fabrics of reverie. The prohibitions of parents and elders and of society in general may be effective in the world of action, but they serve only to enhance the exuberance of thought and the vitality of desire. A healthy compromise between imagination and reality is found by many children in the make-believe of play. The toy is endowed with invisible attributes lavished upon a real object in a solid environment of three dimensions. The rag doll may be more truly beautiful than anything that money can buy from any fine toy store. But as the child grows into and then out of adolescence the scope of make-believe and play becomes progressively smaller, whereas perhaps for that very reason the sweep of imagination vastly exceeds in fertile minds the occasion for real performance in the external environment. A child may speak as a child and play as a child, and in so doing find partial expression for the relentless cerebration within him; but when he becomes a man he must put away childish things. He is a member of an adult community, and must behave in accordance with all of the laws which thereunto appertain.

It is sometimes painful to act like an intelligent and sane adult in a socially correct community. Games of chess or bridge or softball are good pastimes which furnish occasional relaxation, but for the grown-up these games no longer possess the capacity to absorb imagination and exclude reality as do the games of children. An adult who plays like a child is a buffoon. Even in relaxation he must behave in a rational and more or less conventional manner. Every waking hour he plays a part for the benefit of the members of his community, and few there are who can judge from the performance what is going on behind the scenes. The pretense is tiresome and unpleasant, but luckily most people can make it endurable with a "C'est la vie" or a gritting of the teeth or a grimace that may even pass for a smile.

For some poor souls, however, the strain of acting always in accordance with the dictates of the social censor is too great. They break down and behave in a manner that is called irrational, and if they persist in their folly it is generally thought best to have them act out their parts on a stage and in a building erected for their special benefit.

The word "personality" as used by many psychologists today is intended to carry a meaning into which have entered several lines of theory drawn from observations on the conflicts between what an individual would like to do and what his own capacities and limitations and the prohibitions of the social order allow him to do. The concept is related to the original meaning of *persona:* a mask or cloak, the part assumed by an actor on the stage. The mask conceals both from the individual himself and from all those with whom he comes in contact the true nature of his inner feelings and desires. His outward behavior is a compromise which exposes to the public gaze only those restricted desires which meet with the approval of the social censor. This behavior comes to be accepted both by the public and by the performer as the *personality* of the individual. The outward behavior *is* the mask, the part which the individual has learned to play on life's stage. Yet below the surface of personality may be discovered another individual who lives in a hidden world of memories and hopes, an individual not always unlike the one who appears on the stage, but sometimes radically and almost incredibly different.

Every animal organism is driven inexorably in search of goals necessary to sustain life. The vastly greater complexity of the human organism drives man on to the pursuit not only of life, but also of liberty and happiness, power and wealth, social approval and esteem, justice and salvation, self-expression and aggrandizement, affection and admiration, *et cetera ad infinitum*. The list is beyond all reckoning, and in this world beyond all attainment. The scope of man's desire is both his delight and his misery.

Restraint of the emotion bound up with human striving and failure is regarded by modern students of personality as one of the main sources of irritation and unhappiness. If this view is correct, it must follow that any medium for the fulfillment of emotional craving has therapeutic capacity of immense social and practical value. In this capacity resides the unique functional significance of music, for music is a language of emotion in the very special sense that its tonal design is capable of releasing in vicarious fashion the emotions which in ordinary mortals are inexpressible. Yet music has none of the vulgar concomitants and common motives of real emotion. The tertiary qualities of music exist in a realm of ideal and abstract sound. They are pure creation. No other human endeavor or accomplishment is in any way comparable. Everything else in one way or another reflects or portrays *things*. Music is no *thing* at all, yet by a simple paradox it comes out of the most inaccessible and inarticulate regions of human experience and reveals in tonal splendor those things which are closest to the heart of man.

Nothing can express the height and depth and extent of emotion with anything like the artlessness of music. Words, pictures, images, statues, objects, landscapes, portraits, still life: these are all mere things, the outer manifestation of an inner *Ding an sich*. Music on the other hand, said Schopenhauer, is the *Ding an sich* itself. "Music is thus by no means like the other arts, the copy of the Ideas, but the copy of the Will itself, whose objectivity the Ideas are. This is why the effect of music is so much more powerful and penetrating than that of the other arts, for they speak only of shadows, but music speaks of the thing itself." Schopenhauer has not been alone in his half-mystic belief that the master-knot of human fate can be unraveled in only one way, *Solvitur audiendo.*

The function or purpose of music is thus to give alleviating discharge to the inner life of emotion and will, an achievement which is neither an escape nor a flight from reality, as Freud and Adler and some of their followers would have it, but rather a fulfillment and a completion. The emotions and strivings of will and desire are embodied in music not directly, but indirectly by way of tonal designs which closely resemble in formal outline the inner movements of the spirit, the *Gemütsbewegungen.* But here at last it may be true that music becomes symbolic, for it seems to stand for and express the joy and sorrow of all mankind. Tonal ecstasy or grief takes on the meaning of reality, and the listener is profoundly moved, not by his own ecstasy or grief, but by the delight and satisfaction, sometimes almost overpowering, which come from hearing expressed in measured design what he himself could not possibly utter.

———————

Parts of this introduction have appeared in articles published in *The Journal of Aesthetics and Art Criticism* and in a lecture given at the Library of Congress and printed there under the title, "Music as the Language of Emotion." I am grateful for permission to use some of this material and to alter it to suit the purpose of this introduction.

Carroll C. Pratt

The Meaning of Music

The Meaning of Music

A STUDY IN PSYCHOLOGICAL

AESTHETICS

BY

CARROLL C. PRATT

*Assistant Professor of Psychology and Tutor in the Division of
Philosophy in Harvard College*

FIRST EDITION

McGRAW-HILL BOOK COMPANY, Inc.

NEW YORK AND LONDON

1931

The present volume is an elaboration of a few lectures on music given during a course in aesthetics at Harvard University. The main argument is designed to justify the tenacious hold which formalism has had upon musical theory. The argument goes still further and suggests that even the most extreme formalists, by evading the question of emotion in music, have not made their contentions sweeping enough. This topic is dealt with in Part II and in the beginning of Part III. Several sections in these two parts, however, are intended to reveal the inadequacy of any attempt to account for the power of musical sound in terms of a single formula. Part I is given over to certain technicalities which concern the psychologist and aesthetician more than the musician.

Contents

Contents

Part III

THE MEANING OF MUSIC

Part I

The Materials of Music

1. *The Parts of Musical Experience*

For the sake of convenience all musical experience may be divided into three parts. The division is to a certain extent arbitrary inasmuch as the lines of separation can not be clearly drawn, but failure to classify equivocal cases is not sufficient reason for denying real differences where they plainly exist, any more than the difficulties of deciding upon the nature of certain simple protoplasmic structures obliterate the distinction between animals and plants. The divisions of aesthetic experience run parallel to the boundaries which psychology has drawn within mental life as a whole. Just as the stream of consciousness reveals, upon analysis, the flow of sensory, perceptual, and meaningful aspects, so the narrower field of aesthetic experience may be found to contain *material*, *form*, and *expression*. And of music it is also permissible to speak of the material, the form, and the expression.

2. *Material*

By various methods of abstraction and analysis, psychology has been able to come within close range of numerous qualities of experience which have been subsumed under the term sensation. That bits of sensation present themselves in isolation is hardly a tenable doctrine today, but that by appropriate shifts of attention certain sensory aspects of experience may be observed with sufficient accuracy to work out the conditions of their occurrence can be denied by no one. If it were not so, how could colored moving pictures have been developed out of the knowledge furnished by the science of physiological optics? What is true of sensation for general psychology applies with even greater force to material in aesthetics. The material of music is the sensuous stuff of tonal quality in all its gradations and variations. To what extent this sensuous material of music appears in relative isolation is not easy to say, but that all music is saturated with the sensuous element of tonal material simply goes without saying. It is absolutely indispensable to musical form, this lowly sensuous substance of tone, for there can be no form which is not formed out of something. Many who strive after correct taste in art look upon the charm which comes by way of the senses as an inferior mode of perception, forgetting thereby that the fine arts can not exist without their sensory modes and neglecting entirely to justify their ranking of aesthetic pleasures in an order of ethical merit. In music the sensuous element plays a more important part than in almost any other art. Surely in literature, poetry, architecture, sculpture, and even in certain styles of painting, the beauty of material is subordinate to that of form or expression. So it is in music, but not to the same degree. One has only to note the frequent critical comparisons of singers, instrumentalists, orchestras, quartets, choirs, and choruses, on the basis of the quality of tone-production to realize the significance attached to this factor by the sensitive musician or critic.

3. *Form*

If the concept of perception in psychology, or of form in aesthetics, is not examined too critically, its meaning is clear enough. It will be necessary later on to point out some of the difficulties to which the concept has given rise, but a statement of its more obvious meaning will be sufficient for the present. The enumeration of the materials or sensory aspects of experience is merely the first step in psychological description. More immediately apparent to unsophisticated observation than

the materials are the ways in which the materials
are distributed. This arrangement of materials
gives rise to the *formal* or perceptual aspects of
experience, and although form obviously has some
functional relation to the materials, it must nevertheless be borne clearly in mind that form *qua*
form is not to be identified with the structure of
its material parts. Every form has its own unique
quality. The *explanation* of this quality is often to
be sought in the constellation of its parts, but this
explanation, which amounts to a statement of the
conditions which are responsible for the appearance
of the quality, is different from the quality itself.
Failure to recognize this fact is at the root of most
of the trouble in "exact" aesthetics of music.

In many formal qualities the parts are given
phenomenally within the structure itself, and
hence permit of partial explanation in terms of
strictly psychological entities; in other forms the
parts are not given at all. The explanation of such
forms must therefore be given entirely in terms
of the physical properties of the brain and stimulus.
It is probably safe to say that all forms could be
arranged in a linear series extending from one
extreme in which the lack of coherence of the
several parts gives the impression of complexity,
even confusion, to the totality, through an inter-
mediate region in which the forms possess a

unitary character but are nevertheless perceived as made up of parts, to the other extreme in which the form is a complete unit having no phenomenal parts. If this procedure were followed it would, of course, obliterate the difference between sensation and perception, for sensation would then be seen merely as the limiting case of a form which at any one moment of observation revealed no parts.

Many perceptions (tactual and gustatory blends, auditory fusions) likewise present themselves as single unitary affairs, but split up into parts or change their character when attention shifts. Precisely the same situation obtains with the sensation. By a change of attitude the character of a sensation changes: extensity, for example, turns up to replace intensity. There are no psychological experiences whatsoever which, under identical conditions of stimulus, do not change their character when the attitude of the observer varies. The reason is close at hand. Even the simplest phenomenal experiences are the correlates of physical events in which several properties operate simultaneously upon the receptors. Physical amplitude, for example, can not be separated from frequency. The phenomenal correlates, then, of amplitude and frequency are always potentially present, but at any one time only one, or perhaps neither, is actually observed.

For purposes of convenience, however, it is legitimate to make a distinction between sensation and perception, between material and form. Certain experiences are simple and unitary, and can in many cases be marked off easily from those qualities which are complex and multi-membered in structure. For this reason, and also because of the fact that a vast amount of experimental work has been devoted to them, the former deserve a separate grouping of their own, such as is understood in the term sensation. Much less accurately the latter may be comprehended by such a term as perception, but in both cases it is of the utmost importance to remember that the two categories differ not so much in kind as in degree.

It has been conventional, and convenient, to group forms, or perceptions, into three classes: spatial, temporal, and qualitative. The nature of spatial and temporal forms is obvious enough without illustration. Qualitative forms are phenomenally much more subtle and have given no end of trouble to psychological analysis and interpretation. Music furnishes the very best examples of qualitative forms. When the two notes of an octave are sounded together the impression is distinctly unitary, and yet, for the musician at any rate, this unitary impression is always set against a background of two clear parts. Other musical intervals possess different degrees of simultaneous unity and clearness of parts. Each interval, moreover, has its own unique formal character which is not less real by virtue of the inconvenient fact that names for these characters do not lie ready at hand. The fifth is hollow, flat, a bit commonplace; the major third, lively, rich, compact; the major seventh, raspy, bitter, disjointed; *etc*.

To the musician these qualities, although rarely named, are much the most obvious aspects of intervals. To him the fifth is not that tonal relationship with this degree of unity and that degree of clearness of the parts. The fifth is simply the fifth with all of its character of fifthness full upon it. Psychologically these intervals are thought of as qualitative perceptions, or fusions, inasmuch as their unitary character is a matter not of spatial or temporal relations, but of the integration of auditory qualities. As Troland puts it, the unitary character of fusion is a compensation for, or conservation of, the partial losses of identity which are sustained by the parts. An impressive amount of careful experimental work has been done on simple auditory fusions. If the same sort of minute analysis is ever to be made of the tremendously complex harmonies such as are found in Wagnerian scores the lives of many men will have to be devoted to it. Even more important for music than qualitative perceptions are the innumerable varieties of temporal perceptions. Some of these will be considered later.

So important has the rôle of form in music appeared that not a few writers on the subject have maintained vigorously that the whole power of music resides exclusively in its formal structure. In fact, most of the disputes in the aesthetics of music find their origin in the differences between those who place major emphasis on formal properties and those who insist that music transcends the limitations of auditory form and reaches out by way of a subtle language of suggestion and association to a realm of ideas and thoughts no less articulate and intelligible than that in which poetry moves.

4. *Meaning*

Although the meaning of the word "expression" has been well established by Santayana in literature on aesthetics, other meanings in the same literature, to say nothing of loose usage in popular speech, have tended to surround the word with confusion. The frequent inquiries, moreover, as to what a given musical phrase *expresses* complicate matters all the more, for in such questions it

is not at all clear whether the interrogator regards
the expression of a musical phrase as something
psychologically external to the auditory structure
or as a quality intrinsic to the musical material
itself—a difference of no small moment if the
expressiveness of music is the topic of discussion! Without implying that Santayana's use of
the word is any less legitimate than that of Croce,
it would be well to avoid the sharp differences
of definition on the one hand and the careless
ambiguities of usage on the other by falling
back on a word which is much more widely used
in psychological literature to denote the sort of
experience to be dealt with in the third division of
aesthetics, viz., "meaning." The use of this word is
also precarious, but its dangers are fewer, I think,
than those which lurk in the word "expression."

"Meaning" may be defined as those qualities
which reveal no correspondence with the physical
properties of the stimulus. The mind is ever alert
to resemblances and differences, either vague or
clear, which a given object shows to other objects.
These qualities of other objects come in time to
attach themselves as integral properties of the
original object so that the latter thus acquires a
richness of content which it formerly did not possess. This acquisition of content by way of similarity and difference is chiefly responsible for the

lack of correspondence between the stimulus and the impression which it creates, so that another way of stating the above definition would be to say that meanings are those qualities which have been acquired by an object through association and suggestion. An example or two will perhaps indicate more clearly what is meant.

The accompanying figure offers a very simple visual form which, for most people, has little meaning. If, however, one is told that the figure represents a soldier disappearing through a door with a gun over his shoulder and a dog following at his heels, it is obvious at once that when such a figure is seen again it will have a meaning which it did not possess at first. Similarly, for most persons the melodic figure represented by the notes on the staff would not be heavy with signifi-

cance. But for boys playing baseball in back lots bounded by a fence the whistling of these seven notes is, or was at one time, expressive of a more unlucky concrete fate than the most tragic Wagnerian *Leitmotiv*. The fact that the phrase is anything but tragic in its own right only serves to illustrate the way in which greatly dissimilar items may be joined by association.

So baffling and discordant have been the results from experimental studies of meaning that many textbooks of psychology circumvent the topic whenever possible. Some psychologists conveniently sidestep the problem altogether by maintaining in all seriousness that the topic of meaning does not belong to psychology. Such an ostrichlike procedure is deplorable. The present volume is no place for the nice balancing of various bits of evidence which lead to conflicting theories of meaning. It is perhaps pertinent to suggest, however, that certain trends in psychology have unnecessarily befogged the issue of meaning by spreading the concept indiscriminately over nearly the whole surface of phenomenal experience.

We have said that meanings characterize experiences which reveal qualities extraneous to their intrinsic nature. "A fact has a *meaning* when it stands for something else, as a vertical cross for addition. A fact *means* whatever it points to or leads to beyond itself."[1] Let it be proposed that the phrase "intrinsic nature" shall comprehend those properties of an experience which exhibit, or, in the absence of direct evidence, very conceivably might exhibit, some sort of functional relationship

[1] W. E. HOCKING, *Types of Philosophy*, 1929, 99.

to the physical aspects of the stimulus. Such a view does not involve an acceptance of the much discussed "constancy-hypothesis," if by that concept is meant a point-to-point correspondence with the stimulus. But the denial of a one-to-one correlation is not the same thing as the denial of all correlation. It is, of course, a platitude to state that the final mathematical formulation of the conditions which underlie any phenomenal event will perforce include events in the brain-field, but in view of the large gaps of knowledge in the latter domain the only recourse for psychology, in many cases, is the stimulus-field. In spite of the complications introduced by nervous excitation it is not a matter of indifference what the stimulus happens to be!

If the two eyes are stimulated by two properly distributed sources of light each of $700\mu\mu$ the field of vision includes green as well as red. Now although the immediate determinant of this green lies in the central stage of the psychophysiological process, somewhere in the region between the sensory and motor projection-zones of the cerebral cortex,[2] it is at the same time possible to state the

[2] The physical factors which show perfect correlation with corresponding properties of consciousness are referred to by Troland as the direct determinants of consciousness, as contrasted with antecedent stages in the total psychophysical process: the physical object, the stimulus, the

conditions for the appearance of this green with considerable accuracy in terms of location of wavelengths in space, for if either of these factors is altered the green itself changes. In the case, however, of the two illustrations of meaning cited in the preceding paragraph it is at once obvious that although the physical properties of the stimuli have entered into functional relation with the direct physiological determinants of the meanings, these particular physical properties are not the essential conditions of the determinants. Almost any other constellation of stimuli might serve just as well to take over this function. Language is a striking example of the independence of stimulus and meaning. The physical properties of the stimulus-word *red* are by no means essential to

---

sense-organ process, the receptor process, the afferent nerve stimulation, and the afferent nerve conduction, which are called indirect determinants. *Cf.* L. T. TROLAND, *Psychophysiology*, 1929, Vol. I, 148–205. According to this view the stimulus lies in a relatively remote region of determination. In much of his laboratory work, however, the psychologist is unfortunately forced to confine himself to the relations between stimulus and consciousness, or between stimulus and response. Indirect and imperfect as these relations must always be, they nevertheless constitute the most accessible domain for experimentation and furnish the points of departure for investigations into the nature of physiological process.

the meaning. Rosso, bomvu, rouge, qyrmyzy, rot, vörös, rojo, vermelho, ruber, ἐρυθρός, ·—· · —··, rood, raudr, czerwony, אדום, dazeggagh, красный, and pukiki would all do just as well. It is therefore plain enough that certain properties of experience are not functionally related to the stimulus, while certain others just as plainly are.

The difference between experiences which are functionally related to the stimulus and those which are not is not one which is given within experience itself. At the level of experience itself everything is meaningful in the sense that all things possess their own significant characteristics. How has it come about then that psychology has found itself with a problem of meaning on its hands? Various reasons may be given, among which the following are of chief significance.

In the first place, the existence of a psychological problem (like meaning) does not necessarily presuppose that the origin of the problem is within the psychological material itself. Psychophysics is the study of the relation between stimulus and sensation, but this relation is not given within sensation. Once the discovery has been made that sensation varies with certain physical properties, which properties are not, it must be remembered, delivered up to sensation, then the problem of more accurate statement of this variation is fairly launched. More cogent reasons, however, may be found for the intricate development of the problem of meaning.

One of the central problems of philosophy has been, and probably always will be, the relation between body and mind. How is mind, an immaterial, non-extended substance, related to body, which possesses the attributes of materiality and extension? The answers which many philosophers have given to this question have introduced lamentable confusion into psychology. Psychologically, mind is *not* an immaterial, non-extended substance. If mind is whatever one is immediately aware of in his own direct experience (and how else can it be defined?) then extension and materiality (solidity and resistance to pressure) enter directly into this awareness. A glance at the sky or a hard kick against a big stone will convince anyone of these facts. Whether body really has materiality and extension is the only question open to doubt, for body (as a physical object) does not come into direct experience, hence its extension or lack of it must be gotten at by scientific inference and hypothesis. The question, then, how mind can be aware of extension is answered, for psychology, merely by pointing out that extension is one of the attributes of mind, along with materiality and numerous other qualities.

That the same sort of confusion has arisen in psychology itself is even more unfortunate. Brentano and Wundt both had a great deal to do with the raising of much dust with respect to the problem of "reference to an object," or meaning. Characteristic of all psychic phenomena, said Brentano, is their reference to an object. Here again it must be pointed out that except in very special conditions no such *reference* exists in perceiving an object. When I see a tree I certainly am not aware in any way whatever of special "contents" of mind which presently, by virtue of an "act" of reference, acquire the meaning of an object "out there." The tree, as a phenomenal object, is directly given in a certain spatial position. How it comes about that I think of the tree as an object capable of existence apart from my perception of it is a problem irrelevant to the particular topic under discussion. Nor is the position here set forth intended as a denial of the existence of mental acts in general. No implications regarding Brentano's system as a whole or regarding various other psychological and philosophical problems are involved,—merely the assertion that unsophisticated observation is directly opposed to the belief that the simple perception of an object entails a process of reference. It is at least open to doubt that all psychic phenomena are characterized by their reference to an object.

Wundtian psychology, particularly in the hands of Titchener, is equally misleading in its treatment of the problem of meaning. The context-theory of meaning, if it were reserved strictly for those cases in which one idea calls forth another idea, would appear to be an accurate enough account of the course of events, and would be indistinguishable from associationism pure and simple. "One mental process is the meaning of another mental process if it is that other's context. And context, in this sense, is simply the mental process which accrues to the given process through the situation in which the organism finds itself."[3] But for Titchener a mental process is not an idea, not a meaning. He argues

. . . that mental processes do not intrinsically mean, that meaning is not a constituent part of their nature . . . You may not have realized positively and intimately, that sensations and simple images are all meaningless; that we have described them simply as processes, as experiences going on . . . there is, however, no real difficulty, when once these things are pointed out, in taking up a scientific standpoint towards the mental elements.[4]

[3] E. B. TITCHENER, *A Text-book of Psychology*, 1910, 367.
[4] E. B. TITCHENER, *A Beginner's Psychology*, 1915, 30, 90.

Now if one bears in mind that meaning is not a property of mental process, then the context-theory reduces to this: one mental process (which by definition has no meaning) is the meaning of another mental process (which, again, is without meaning) if it is that other's context. When regarded in this light it is not at all clear how the mere juxtaposition of two meaningless processes constitutes a meaningful experience. The theory encounters still greater difficulty if one considers again the perception of a tree. For Titchener such a perception must obviously be a meaning. But where, in seeing a tree, does one look for the two meaningless processes one of which is the context for the other? Ordinarily the tree is seen as a unitary object, which, however, is susceptible of easy division into parts, such as the trunk, branches, and leaves. But these parts themselves are all meanings. If analysis is carried still further one may single out such aspects as the color or height, and if the abstraction has gone so far that one perceives not the color *of the tree* nor the height *of the tree*, but simply sheer color and height, then the tree itself has gone, and the original problem presents itself again. How can meaningless quality and meaningless extension make a meaningful tree? The difficulty of the problem is increased by recent evidence which tends to show that even under ideal conditions of laboratory observation two such simple processes as the above cannot exist together simultaneously with sufficient clearness to be reported upon accurately, so that if attention is directed to the color the reports upon extension amount to little more than guesses of varying degrees of inaccuracy.[5]

In all fairness it must be admitted that the above question about two meaningless processes making a meaning is in the nature of a quibble, but a quibble to which the statement of the context-theory lays itself open. As a matter of fact, it is impossible to talk about two processes *together* in terms of the character which each possessed when taken in isolation, for when they are together they are different from what they were when they were apart. If this difference is what Titchener refers to as a meaning, then certain of the objections to the context-theory fall away. But one must read a good deal into the context-theory to satisfy himself that this change due to sensory combination is intended to be a meaning. Changes such as these in the *nucleus* of a perception are dealt with under the rubrics of qualitative, durative, and extensive

[5] *Cf.* E. G. BORING's report on an experiment by YOKO-YAMA, *American Journal of Psychology*, 1924, 35, 301*ff.*; and O. KÜLPE, "Versuche über Abstraktion," *I. Kongress für experimentelle Psychologie*, 1904, 56–68.

attributes of perception, whereas "the processes which *surround* the nucleus carry the meaning."[6] All too frequently in Titchener's psychology meanings are synonymous with the stimulus-objects to which mental process supposedly refers. "Every teacher of experimental psychology knows how difficult it is to dissociate sensation from meaning (*i.e.*, from stimulus) in the beginner's mind."[7]

We are constantly confusing sensations with their stimuli, with their objects, with their meanings . . . We do not say, in ordinary conversation, that this visual sensation is lighter than that, but that this pair of gloves or this kind of grey note-paper is lighter than this other. We do not say that this complex of cutaneous and organic sensations is more intensive than that, but that this box or package is heavier than this other. We do not even say, as a rule, that this tonal quality is lower than that, but rather that this instrument is flat and must be tuned up to this other. Always in what we say there is a reference to the objects, to the meaning of the conscious complex. It is not grey, pressure, tone, that we are thinking of; but the grey of leather or paper, the pressure of the box, the pitch of the violin. Now the stimuli, the physical processes, are magnitudes or quantities. What is more natural, then, than to say that the corresponding grey or pressure or tone is also a magnitude or a quantity? What is more natural than to

[6] E. B. TITCHENER, *Beginner's Psychology*, 118. Italics mine.

[7] E. B. TITCHENER, *Experimental Psychology*, 1905, Vol. II, pt. II, lxiv.

read the character of the stimuli, of the objects, into the "sensations" with which certain aspects of stimulus or object are correlated?[8]

Throughout the Wundtian psychology one meets the old confusion of the body-mind problem reformulated in terms of *process* and *meaning*. Trees, houses, tables, chairs: these are all meanings, and if the psychologist describes his experience with reference to these objects he is accused of committing what Titchener was fond of calling the "stimulus-error." That is to say, these objects are physical events (stimuli), whereas the psychologist must confine himself to mental events. Against this view it must simply be urged that these objects, as given in perception, are not physical events. Whether they are meanings or not is purely a matter of definition, but more serious questions than mere verbal definition are raised when they are excluded from psychology on the ground that they belong in the same category with molecules, atoms, electrons, protons, wave-lengths, electromagnetic fields, *etc*. The same confusion occasionally leads Bentley to thrust certain psychological experience into another order of existence.

It scarcely seems possible that such things as books and violins should be mistaken for the furnishings of the mind;

[8] *Ibid.*, pt. I, xxvi.

but this is precisely the first error that the beginner drops into in his quest for component qualities . . . Just so soon as you find that you are regarding your object either as something which has a permanent existence or which is a part of a physical order, so soon you may be certain that you have not brought under your observation a mental object at all, but instead something which belongs to another order of existence.[9]

One is tempted to ask Bentley how books and violins, if they belong to another order of existence, can be brought under one's observation.[10] The fact that they are *regarded* as having a permanent existence or as belonging to a physical order does not actually make them permanent or lend to them a status in the physical order. It merely gives to them another meaning.

That these objects may very properly be defined as psychological meanings no one can possibly gainsay. They belong somewhere in the field of psychology, but their classification is always more or less arbitrary and is made largely for the sake of convenience of handling. In the belief that it will

[9] M. BENTLEY, *The Field of Psychology*, 1924, 36f.

[10] The same question can be put with respect to the physicist's observation of electrons. I am not sure what the answer to this question is, but I am perfectly certain that books and violins come directly into my field of observation, whereas molecules and atoms do not.

make for clarity of exposition, an attempt will be made in these pages to restrict more narrowly the field of meaning, and to define it, as has already been done above, as any experience which reveals properties extraneous to itself, or as an object which points to or stands for another object. This use of the term is in harmony with its most frequent meaning in ordinary speech, and corresponds to one of the three uses which Miss Calkins finds least objectionable among the seven main technical senses in which the word has been employed.[11]

[11] M. W. CALKINS, "The Ambiguous Concept; Meaning," *American Journal Psychology*, 1927, 39, 7–22. Miss Calkins writes in the hope that she may persuade here and there a psychologist to expel the word "meaning" from his professional vocabulary. Sound as this advice is, in extenuation of the continued use of the term it may be noted that if psychology were to banish all ambiguous terms from its vocabulary it would have to develop a complete system of symbols such as those used in mathematical logic. In the absence of such a system the next best thing to do is to state the sense in which a word is being used and try not to depart from that usage. Moreover, one of the purposes of the present book is to suggest an answer to the frequently repeated question, What is the meaning of music? In that question, as contrasted with inquiries regarding the *expression* of music, the word is used, I think, exactly as defined in the text, *viz.*, what does music present to the mind in addition to the content of the auditory structure itself, or, in other words, what does music point to beyond itself?

Now in our example of the tree it has been argued that the perception of such an object does not necessarily involve any of the three following complications: (1) the perception of properties other than those showing some sort of correlation with the physical properties of the tree, (2) the reference to some object other than the tree itself, or (3) the tying together of simpler psychological processes. What, then, is the perception of an object?

The perception of an object is simply the perception of a sensory *form*. Under the best conditions of laboratory observation it is possible to get sensory material almost completely stripped of formal properties, but under ordinary conditions of observation the forms or patterns of sensory material are more obvious, and certainly more important for the business of finding one's way about in the world, than the sensory material itself. The form, moreover, varies independently of the material. A circle is a circle whether it be black, white, red, orange, yellow, green, blue, or violet. A melody is recognized as the same melody no matter which of the twelve keys it is played in. To the extent, then, that sensory material, conditioned by specific physical properties of the stimulus, assumes a definite form, which in turn is conditioned by temporal and spatial arrangements of these properties, it is not legitimate to speak of a meaning in the sense defined above.

The mere naming of a sensory experience does not create its form (nor its meaning) any more than the allocation of the letters r-e-d to a color gives to the color its redness. The form of a tree is independent of language as well as of subsequent uses and properties which come to be associated with it. A tree, in addition to being a certain formal sensory structure, is also an object which may be climbed, chopped down with an axe, or pruned for better growth, and the perception of the relations which the tree may bear to other events will bring it about that additional properties accrue to those contained in the original perception, but it must be insisted that pruning, felling, and climbing are not essential to the formal structure.

It would be platitudinous to labor this point were it not for the fact that such perceptual forms have frequently been treated as though they were meanings in the sense of experiences which have developed by way of contextual supplementation to a sensory core or nucleus—as though the circularity of a red circle were an image added on to the red and therefore less intrinsic to the perception of the circle than the redness. It must, on the contrary, be obvious that circularity in such an experience is given just as immediately as redness, and it can be demonstrated, furthermore, that it depends for its form on the points of origin of the sheaf of light-rays which converge upon the nodal point of the eye. Between the latter physical properties and the structure of the visual field there is, of course, no identity but merely a correlation. (An areal magnitude of 1,700 million miles at a distance of one light-year presents a barely perceptible speck in the visual field.) But the fact of correlation is sufficient to establish the functional dependence of visual form upon the stimulus—no less in the case of a tree than in that of a circle.

Although, strictly speaking, there can be no sensory material which is without form and void, and hence no point to the question whether one is prior to the other, it nevertheless remains true that at any moment of experience one is likely to be subordinate to the other, sometimes to the point of the latter's complete disappearance. An observer who is set in the laboratory to report upon the form of an object presented tachistoscopically is frequently unable to make any judgment whatever as to its color. I have seen a baby whose experience with gloves was limited to small red mittens try to put its hands into a pair of large gray gloves. The crucial item in directing such behavior must surely have been the form rather than the color or size. Recent experiments with children tend to give support to such observations. Each child was shown two small objects, for example, a sphere and a cube. A third object was then introduced which resembled one of the first two objects in color and the other in form, and the child was asked which of the first two objects the third one was most like. With children from two to three the objects were matched almost always by form, from three to six more frequently by color, and from six to the adult level again more often by form.[12] Whatever may be the interpretation of these results they support, at all events, observations made with adults in the laboratory to the effect that color and form may operate under certain circumstances with relative independence.

This long digression into the problem of meaning has been risked in order not only to point out certain of the intricacies of the problem but more especially to argue that many experiences which have been classified as meanings, and therefore treated as though they involved a pointing-to relation or a tying together of simpler processes, more accurately belong under the heading of form. If an intelligible answer is to be given to the ques-

[12] C. R. BRIAN and F. L. GOODENOUGH, "The Relative Potency of Color and Form Perception at Various Ages," *Journal of Experimental Psychology*, 1929, 12, 197–213.

tion of formalism and expressionism in music, the question itself must be framed in such a way that the terms form and expression (meaning) are not too hopelessly confused. Expression, as a special case of meaning as defined above, is frequently regarded as the most salient characteristic of music. This view will be examined later. For the present it is enough to mark off by definition the realm of meaning from that of form, realizing, of course, that no sharp line of division separates them, but that some attempt at separation is absolutely necessary if the opposing claims of two great schools on the aesthetics of music are to be understood.

5. *Justification for Division into Parts*

Of late it has become fashionable to deprecate analysis of experience into parts on the ground that the quality of experience can only be apprehended in its totality. If understood correctly, there is one sense in which such a view is tenable, but to leap from this position to the extremity of denying the validity of all analysis is wholly unwarranted. Misunderstanding of the strictures leveled against certain kinds of associationism by *Gestalttheorie*, a new movement in German psychology, is responsible for much of the prattle about the unanalyzable wholeness of totalities. If a given experience, under the same conditions of stimulation and under introspective analysis, reveals parts, aspects, and abstractions, a description of these items constitutes perfectly sound psychological technique. It is the subsequent interpretation of the relation of these items to the original whole that causes the trouble. But to deny that these items may exist is equivalent to saying that a keen ear can not hear out the quality of the bass clarinet in a full orchestra. The last word on the relation of parts to whole, and *vice versa*, has by no means been said, and certainly no attempt will be made to say it here, but it will be necessary to take up a position on the matter a little later in connection with the characteristics of musical material and form.

The division of aesthetic experience into material, form, and meaning has also been viewed sceptically for much the same reason, *viz.*, that a work of art is a totality and can only be adequately grasped in its totality. Now it may be granted without argument that the aesthetic experience generally presents a totality, a coherence of parts, an integrality, a wholeness, a structural unity, or what not. But it must be remembered that quite apart from the question of whether such unitary experiences reveal or contain parts the inescapable fact remains that given the same stimulus one person may perceive a totality very appreciably different from that perceived by another person, and that the difference between these two experiences may coincide exactly with that which characterizes the difference between material and form, or between one form and another. And the same person, at different times, may derive very different experiences from the same stimulus, and descriptions of these differences would reveal now form, now meaning as the salient feature of the totality. In treating of the stimulus apart from its variations in individual experience it is therefore legitimate to draw such distinctions. Santayana's division of aesthetic experience into material, form, and expression has recently been objected to by Katherine Gilbert on the ground that his explanation of the total effect in terms of these parts is insecurely founded on mistaken theory.

"A striking proof of the compound nature of tragic effects," he [Santayana] says, "can be given by a simple experiment. Remove from any drama—say from *Othello*—the charm of the medium of expression; reduce the tragedy to a mere account of the facts and of the words spoken, such as our newspapers almost daily contain; and the tragic dignity and beauty is entirely lost. Nothing remains but a disheartening item of human folly, which may still excite curiosity, but which will rather defile than purify the mind that considers it."

Without at this point prejudicing the issue of our argument, we may yet indicate for purposes of clarification that in any aesthetics of expression, conventionally so-called, this crucial experiment would be regarded as a monstrous proposal and as the *reductio ad absurdum* of the method that allowed it. Many philosophers would say that the supposition that you can abstract the medium from a work of art and have a recognizable part of it left is insecurely founded on mistaken theory.[13]

It matters not how many philosophers say that the supposition that the medium may be abstracted from a work of art is insecurely founded on mistaken theory, the psychologist must insist that such abstraction is entirely possible and rests securely on correct fact. For many people who find themselves exposed to Shakespere, the poet's sensuous medium is so far off in the margin of consciousness that it might just as well not be present at all as far as contributing any charm is concerned; for others the beauty of poetic structure and form fails completely of realization; and for those who do not understand the English language the sound of the words carries no meaning. Surely every teacher of poetry and drama would subscribe to such statements. Why does the philosopher not believe them? Again, at least in the case of Mrs. Gilbert, it looks as though the old confusion of the

[13] K. GILBERT, *Studies in Recent Aesthetic*, 1927, 120.

body-mind problem were at fault. Shakespere's *Othello*, if one is to speak of it as an event which is independent of anyone's experience of it, must be described in terms of the physical properties which underlie black symbols on a page or sounds of the human voice. When these physical properties are brought into relation with the physiological processes of a human nervous system, they may or may not deliver to consciousness a structure which includes a clear sensuous medium. They may or may not have form; they may or may not be interpreted alike by different people (was Hamlet mad?); they may or may not give rise to vast stretches of associative imagery; *etc*.

Tragic effects *are* compound in their nature, not, perhaps, at the level of experience itself, but certainly in their underlying conditions, physical, physiological, and sometimes psychological. "It would not be the story of Shakespere's *Othello*, or any component of it, so the argument would run, that would be left after the removal of Shakespere's verse and architecture."[14] What does Mrs. Gilbert mean, in this sentence, by "Shakespere's *Othello*"? If she refers to the physical properties of the printed page, then the substitution for these of the physical properties of a newspaper page containing a reporter's account of a murder would most cer-

[14] *Ibid.*, 120*f*.

tainly be interfering with Shakespere. But from the context it seems more likely that she refers to Shakespere's *Othello* as an *experienced* object, in which case it must again be pointed out that the experience of *Othello* may undergo all manner of variations without in the least disturbing the identity of the play. It is *not* a monstrous proposal nor a *reductio ad absurdam* to speak of the removal from such an experience of the verse or of the architecture or of the sensuous medium. Such removals are constantly being accomplished by shifts in attention or by differences in physiological make-up of the individuals having the experience.

The point at issue is important enough to warrant further exposition by means of a simple example. In the experiments of Külpe mentioned above, observers were shown for a very brief interval a piece of paper on which were drawn, at various positions, forms (circles, diamonds, squares, *etc.*) of different colors. For purposes of convenience the items on the piece of paper may be regarded as physical events independent of the observers, although for such purposes they should, of course, be described in terms of the radiant energy of light-waves. Now if, before the exposure, the observer is told to report the colors he sees, his account will be fairly accurate. If, however, he is then asked to state in what forms the colors appeared, his report will show many inaccuracies. He may even be completely unaware of the existence of any definite forms at all. If, on the other hand, he is instructed, before the exposure, to make a report on the forms, his account of the colors or the location of the forms will be very incomplete. If he is given no instructions at all, the experience which he has will depend on the particular physiological "set" of the moment, and his description of the experience will show that certain psychological properties generally correlated with the physical events were either not present at all or were so far off in the margin of consciousness that they might just as well have been absent. Given such a stimulus an observer will discover (on different presentations of the same stimulus) various properties: color, form, size, extent, similarities or differences between the forms or colors, spatial location, affective qualities, and even associated meanings—although such stimuli are designed to eliminate the elaborate associations to which pictures or words would ordinarily give rise. But at any one time not all of these properties would by any means be present.

From such facts as these it is therefore perfectly legitimate to insist that in a complicated work like *Othello* not all of the potential properties are present during a given presentation. After repetition more and more properties are delivered up to consciousness and these come, in time, to be regarded as permanent characteristics of the Shakesperian drama, no matter how many or how few of them may actually come within the range of attention during a single performance, so that the individual who is uncommonly sensitive to poetic and dramatic values speaks of a play with which he is very familiar in terms of all the characteristics which it has ever revealed to him. This manner of speaking must not, however, obscure the psychological fact that these characteristics do not all function simultaneously at the level of experience. Experientially they may and do function independently, and it is this independent variability of properties which are discovered to belong to the same *physical* object which justifies the division of experience into parts.

The question as to how many of the characteristics which appear upon successive presentations of the same stimulus may properly be ascribed to the original experience is an exceedingly difficult one to answer, and no apology will be made for circumventing it wherever possible in these pages. In the early days of experimental psychology the practice was consistently followed of presenting the same stimulus over and over again for purposes of psychological description, and then putting these piecemeal descriptions together to stand as the total mosaic. Some of the dire consequences of this procedure, particularly in the field of music, will be dwelt upon later. On the other hand, it is not at all clear beyond doubt that the opposite extreme, advocated in many quarters today, will furnish psychology with its methodological utopia, *viz.*, the view that every experience is a unique totality and resistant at all points to analysis into parts.

To what extent items which were not immediately observable at first glance, but which turn up presently as *somehow* intimately mixed up with the same experience, may correctly be regarded as parts of the whole is a matter which sadly needs careful investigation. Until some happy resolution of the difficulty is arrived at, it is best simply to recognize the problem, and then avoid its complications as far as possible. We shall assume, for the most part, that the problematic relation to an experience of items which are subsequently observed may best be envisaged as one of *physiological determination*. That is to say, those items which were only noted on later repetitions of the same stimulus could not, in all probability, have been present during the original experience, and hence cannot be regarded as *psychological* determinants of the experience. Inasmuch, however, as they are correlated with the same stimulus which was operating during the original experience, it is reasonable to assume that they may be taken as an index of the underlying physiological processes set into operation by the stimulus. Only a few of these processes at any given moment are effective at the level of experience itself, but the nature of these processes, and hence the experience itself, must in part be determined by the other processes in which they are embedded. From this point of view every experience is unique in the sense that it cannot be described in terms of subsequent properties correlated with the same stimulus, but the physiological *explanation* of the experience assumes the form of a deduction based on the complete array of properties correlated with the stimulus. This interpretation of the rôle of analysis in psychology is in line with certain concepts of *Gestalttheorie*, and also has many points in common with the view suggested by Santayana over thirty years ago in defense of his division of aesthetic experience into parts.

In distinguishing, then, in our sense of beauty, an appreciation of sensible material, one of abstract form, and another of associated values, we have been merely following the established method of psychology, the only one by which it is possible to analyze the mind. We have distinguished the elements of the object, and treated the feeling as if it were composed of corresponding parts . . . But aesthetic feeling has no parts, and this *physiology of its causes* is not a description of its proper nature.[15]

Whether by the phrase "physiology of its causes" Santayana meant exactly the type of explanation referred to above is difficult to say, for he does not expand the view, but it is certainly clear that he was alive to the fact that the description of an event is not the same as its explanation— a fact which psychologists frequently lose sight of, as we shall see later.

Given a psychological event A, there are various procedures which may be resorted to in studying that event scientifically. One method is to repeat the stimulus for A several times for purposes of description of the correlated experiences. These several descriptions may be called a, b, c, d, and e. We have already seen that it is a very dubious procedure to assume that A is made up of a, b, c, d, and e. It is much safer to assume that a, b, c, d, and e are the phenomenal correlates of the physiological processes, a', b', c', d', and e', which underlie the event A. Further physiological processes which are not reflected at all in experience may be called f, g, h, and i, and the physical

[15] G. SANTAYANA, *The Sense of Beauty*, 1896, 267. Italics mine.

properties of the stimulus may be designated as j, k, l, m, and n. In our present state of knowledge the best explanation of A would have to be couched in terms both of observed correlations and of hypothetical correlations between A and all of the variables, a', b', c', d', e', f, g, h, i, j, k, l, m, and n. As a matter of fact, since many of these correlations are extremely hypothetical (although at the same time highly probable), most explanations in psychology confine themselves to the statement of the observed relations between A and a group of the physical variables, k, l, and m, usually referred to simply as the *stimulus*. The assumption is, however, that eventually within the region of direct physiological determination some variable, h, will be found which will show a perfect correlation with A. The final explanation of A will then be given in terms of the relation h-A. Why A should be the invariable correlate of h is not, of course, within the power of psychology, or any other science, for that matter, to answer; and any philosophy which professes to do more or hurls abuse at psychology for doing less must furnish convincing evidence that its arrogance is justified or that the modesty of psychology is false.

Let it be noted, finally, that nowhere among these physical and physiological variables which are regarded as the *conditions* for the event A

does the event A itself put in an appearance. A is a unique experience and its proper nature is obviously not identical with any of its conditions. Redness, in other words, is not identical with any of its physical or physiological conditions. Not a few writers, however, have reproached psychology with the bizarre argument that since mental qualities (like redness) are not found in nature (with a capital N) then mind (with a capital M) is different from nature and *therefore* cannot be explained by reference to nature! Such obdurate refusal to note the distinction between the *description* and the *explanation* of an event is only an extreme instance of the confusion which all too frequently appears in the literature on the subject to which, after this long prelude, we shall now turn directly.

6. *The Materials of Music*

The world of sound may be divided roughly into three groups: vocables, noises, and tones. These groups acquire their relative independence in a threefold manner. Each one has a salient feature which is much less marked in the other two groups. Noises and vocables, for example, both have a trace of pitch, but not nearly in so palpable a degree as do tones. Each group, moreover, is set off from the others through the context in

which it is generally found—tones in music,
vocables in human speech, and noises in the
material world. And lastly, each group has its own
unique relation to the physical properties of the
stimulus. Vocables and noises, fascinating as they
are in their own right and tempting as it is to
linger over them awhile, and closely related as they
often are to music, need not detain us. Music is
made of tonal stuff, and to tones we must accordingly give passing attention. But so thoroughly
and adequately has the subject of tone been
treated in other places that it would be purposeless
duplication to go over the ground again in these
pages.[16] Only those characteristics of tone will be
touched upon which are of especial significance in
understanding the treatment of musical form and
meaning.

Psychologists have frequently adopted the practice of characterizing a simple sensory phenomenon
by reference to its attributes. Much controversy
has arisen in recent years over the question of

[16] Excellent accounts and bibliographies of auditory
phenomena may be found in D. C. MILLER, *The Science of
Musical Sounds*, 1915; R. M. OGDEN, *Hearing*, 1924; and
J. REDFIELD, *Music: a Science and an Art*, 1928. The reader
should also be referred, of course, to that great masterpiece
of scientific inquiry, H. HELMHOLTZ, *Sensations of Tone*,
trans. with appendix by A. J. Ellis, 2d ed., 1885.

attributes because of the older psychologists'
corollary that the sum of the attributes constituted
a sensory element called the sensation, a view which
at the present time finds little favor. But the facts
on which this view was based are sound enough,
even if their interpretation is dubious. A sensory
experience, like a tone, may, under identical conditions of stimulation, be listened to from a limited
number of different attitudes, and each of these
attitudes yields a different sort of sensory quality
or attribute.

These qualities, or dimensions, as they are
coming to be called by some writers, are regarded
as the basic channels through which the stream
of sensory stuff flows. Certain of these dimensions, such as intensity and duration, are characteristic of all sensory phenomena in all sense
departments and are obvious enough in their
meaning to warrant passing over them without
further consideration at this point. The qualitative
dimensions, however, although found, of course, in
each sense department, are all different from each
other and give to the several senses their distinctive
features. Only under the most highly specialized
conditions of laboratory observation do these
dimensions appear in anything approximating even
relative isolation, but for purposes of description
they may be treated apart from their interrelations

and their formal properties. The sensuous stuff of music, the materials of music, are, from the psychological point of view, coincident with the sensory dimensions of tone.

7. Pitch

For musical purposes the most striking characteristic of tones is their pitch. The origin of the meaning of this word in the English language is obscure, whereas the corresponding words in German and French (*Höhe* and *hauteur*) obviously refer directly to the characteristics which are only derived meanings in the word "pitch," *viz.*, the positions which tones occupy on a scale running from low to high. The physical correlate of pitch is the frequency of pendular motion of some elastic medium (usually air) set into vibration by various kinds of oscillating bodies. If the form of the pendular motion is simple the tone is called *pure*. Introduction of complexities in the form of motion produces differences in the timbre, or what musicians call the *quality* of the tone.

The range of frequencies to which the human ear is sensitive reaches from about 20 to 20,000 vibrations per second. In the upper reaches the discrimination of pitch is very uncertain and has not been studied accurately enough to warrant any dogmatic assertions that the apparent discriminations are actually made on the basis of pitch. It is not at all impossible that discriminations of pitch in these very high regions are actually based on extraneous noise-components or differences in intensity. At all events, these very high tones are of no value, or at least are not used, in music. The highest note of the pipe organ has the pitch 8,448, and the orchestral piccolo falls short of 5,000. At the other end of the scale music makes use of tones much nearer the lower limit of hearing. The lowest note of the grand piano is 27.5; of the orchestral double bass, 41.2; and of a large pipe organ, 16. Since determinations of the lower limit of audition vary from 12 to 20, or a little higher, it can be seen that the low C of 32 foot (or stopped 16 foot) organ pedal pipes, which produce a tone of only 16 vibrations per second, is in a critical region as far as tone quality is concerned. The value of these tones lies rather in the volumic support which they give to the upper registers than in their pitch. This must obviously be the case in those few organs which have 64 foot pedal pipes.

The number of discriminable pitches between 20 and 20,000 is, of course, much larger than that which ever enters the realm of music. The exact number, however, is very difficult to determine accurately. Older estimates yielded a figure in the vicinity of 11,000. More recent and much more accurate studies of the problem tend to reduce this figure drastically. Discrepancies in numbers arrived at by different investigators are due to various factors other than the intrinsic difficulty of the problem itself: widely different methods of observation and calculation, lack of agreement as to the definition of a just noticeable difference, differences in timbre and intensity of pitches used, *etc*. Since, however, the question is not of vital significance for music, these technicalities of experimental procedure may be passed over. Even when some investigators put the figure at less than 3,000, it is clear at once that the number of pitches used in music drops far below that value. The grand piano has 88 notes, 88 different pitches. A large pipe organ has some 120 different pitches.

In the middle region of the musical scale a semitone, the smallest pitch-difference used in music, is over twenty times as large as the smallest difference which the ear can detect. Does this mean that music is missing its opportunities to the extent of some 2,000 tones? The advocates of quarter-, eighth-, and sixteenth-tone music, pointing to the discriminatory capacity of the ear beyond the semitone, urge that although it would not be feasible to add 2,000 notes to the musical range, it would be highly desirable to utilize more than 120 pitches. To this question of dividing the semitone for the purpose of giving music larger scope, we shall return later. Let it not be thought, however, in the light of the fine distinctions which the ear can make in tones, that the present resources of musical convention are capable of quick exhaustion by the roaring young lions of ultra-modernistic persuasions. If the number of pure-tone pitches in music is multiplied by their range of intensities and by the timbres of different instruments and organ stops, a conservative estimate of the resulting gradations of pitch, tone-color, and intensities through which musical inventiveness may move would place the figure at not less than 50,000. Not too inconsiderable a choice to put at the disposal of the composer!

An interesting question which has often bothered psychologists is this: Why are high tones called "high" and low tones called "low?" High and low refer to positions in space, whereas differences in pitch are not commonly thought of as spatial in origin. In all sensory phenomena, to be sure, one may detect some degree of spatial orientation. The different sense departments do not, however, have equal shares of spatial material. The sense of hearing has come off rather badly in this respect. Sounds, in spite of their volumic proportions, are not spread out in space, and localization of them frequently reveals curious inaccuracies and vagaries. And yet for the differentiation of certain tonal qualities it becomes necessary to draw upon terms which are very evidently spatial in meaning. The tones at one end of the scale are called high and those at the other end are called low, and changes along this scale are spoken of as rising and falling inflections, ascending or descending cadences, downward or upward movements. The conspicuous fitness of such phrases is immediately apparent.

The application to a given sense impression of adjectives which belong strictly to impressions from other modalities occasions, as a rule, little comment. Colors are called warm and odors heavy not because the psychological thermometers and balances are raised or tipped, but rather because by fairly obvious associations they remind one of experiences in other sense departments. It has not been so simple a matter, however, to discover the associative bond which has led so uniformly to the application of the terms high and low in tonal pitch.

Stumpf has found that adjectives meaning high and low (or words closely related in meaning) have been applied to tones in almost every known language.[17] But why should tones be characterized as high or low? Do these characteristics refer to

[17] C. STUMPF, *Tonpsychologie*, 1883, I, 192 *ff*.

differences in spatial height and depth? The answer
to this second question has been almost without
exception in the negative. These words are merely
figurative, and must be accounted for in terms of
secondary criteria, such as, for example, the apparent localization of high vocal tones in the head and
low ones in the chest. The composer Berlioz makes
sport of such explanations and reminds his readers
that high and low tones for the pianist lie in the
horizontal directions of right and left and that the
violoncellist must reach downward to produce high
tones, and suggests that those composers of opera
who use descending passages for a person falling
downstairs have stupidly transferred to the tones
the arbitrary downward character of the printed
notes on the staff. And yet Stumpf, convinced that
there can be no intrinsic height and depth in tones,
has felt obliged to argue that here again some
associative mechanism, strangely obscure and
elusive, has been at work. Even Wundt was forced
to agree with Stumpf in calling these terms meta-
phorical when applied to tones,[18] and most psychologists who have given the matter any thought
have expressed similar views.

What are the associative bonds or the relations
of similarity which cause tones to be so appro-

[18] W. WUNDT, *Grundzüge der physiologischen Psychologie*,
1910, II, 78.

priately designated as high and low? Stumpf has put himself to great pains to discover possible clues. Since there are no verbal expressions, aside from the letters of the alphabet, for tonal qualities, language has borrowed from various sense departments words which apply to impressions accompanied by feelings similar to those to which tones give rise. Thus the affective character of low tones is gloomy and dark while that of high tones is sharp and bright, even painful in very high tones, as though the ear were pierced by a needle. Low tones give the impression of voluminousness and massiveness as contrasted with the thinness and smallness of high tones. The times for low tones to be fully perceived are longer than those for high tones, with the result that rapid passages in the upper part of the scale seem light and airy while passages at the same tempo in the bass sound heavy, clumsy, and labored.

Even these few examples enable one to discern the associative trail which language has followed in the selection of spatial metaphors for pitch-differences. Thin, small, light, airy: these are terms suitable for objects which, if not always found at high altitudes, are at any rate up and away from the ground. Dark and gloomy objects tend to be nearer the surface of the earth, the massive parts of a structure support the smaller parts, and heavy objects are generally lower in space than light ones.

Such was the explanation Stumpf was forced to adopt, and most psychologists have been inclined to accept his view. Titchener, for example, refers to Stumpf's discussion of the question, and then warns the reader that in the study of tonal sensations he must not be misled by the frequent use of metaphor and analogy; that it is not altogether clear how the adjectives high and low came to be applied to tones, but that it is quite clear that they must not be taken as indicative of a spatial character in pitch.[19]

To account for cross-modality references by means of association appears, in many cases, plausible enough. But the most ingenious arguments from association, even in the hands of Stumpf, fail to carry conviction when applied to tonal height and depth. Some of this doubt finds expression in the reservations which Titchener makes when he says that "It is not altogether easy to see" and "we cannot yet say certainly"[20] how the terms high and low came to be applied to tones. Even in the face of this doubt it is legitimate, of course, to suppose that the associative items which Stumpf and others have mentioned serve in some

[19] E. B. Titchener, *A Text-book of Psychology*, 1910, 94 f.
[20] E. B. Titchener, *A Beginner's Psychology*, 1915, 52.

way to reinforce those tonal properties which lead to spatial characterizations. The doubt attaches rather to explanations couched solely in terms of such items. Does not the universality of spatial characterization point to some factor more fundamental than any which derive from cross-modality analogy and supplementation?

The answer to this question appears very simple if one rids himself of certain old presuppositions and faces the problem anew. Prior to any associative addition there exists in every tone an intrinsic spatial characteristic which leads directly to the recognition of differences in height and depth along the musical scale. This statement is based on results of experiments recently performed in the Harvard Psychological Laboratory with the view to determine what observers would do when asked to localize the position from which a tone seemed to come.[21] These observers were told to locate on a numbered scale running from the floor to the ceiling the position of tones coming from a Western Electric No. 2-A Audiometer. Only at the outset did the observers experience any difficulty with the judgment. The tonal impression seemed at

[21] For the quantitative results, and for the original account (part of which is here reprinted by permission), see my article. "The Spatial Character of High and Low Tones," *Journal of Experimental Psychology*, 1930, 13, 278–285.

93200

first to pervade the whole room, but as the attentional direction fell in line with the task imposed by the instructions this difficulty entirely vanished and the judgments were made easily and quickly, and with surprising consistency. The results were clear-cut and unequivocal.

High tones are phenomenologically higher in space than low ones. Of two tones of different pitch the one of greater frequency is called higher, not because of any extraneous associations with altitude, but simply because it is perceived as occupying a higher position in phenomenological space.

An objection is likely to be raised at this point. May it not be that the observers were not actually making judgments of spatial location, but were merely assigning to clearly recognized differences in pitch the spatial characters which inevitably attach to the terms universally employed to designate these pitch-differences? In other words, an observer calls a tone high in space simply because he recognizes it as high in pitch. In the light of the conviction of the observers it seems that such is emphatically not the case. As soon as one has his attention directed to the spatial property of a tone the phenomenon of pitch-locality becomes very real and unmistakable. Moreover, the pitches used in the experiment all bore the octave-relation to each other. Now it is a well-known fact that confusions of the octave within which a pitch lies are very frequent—a judgment sometimes being off by as much as two or three octaves. One would naturally suppose that if the observers were placing the notes on the basis of pitch-quality the error of octave-confusions (especially since these tones were practically pure) would introduce frequent reversals of localization. But the significant fact is that such reversals rarely occurred. A given pitch was placed always very close to the same point.

These results possess obvious implications and consequences. If they receive further verification, auditory theory must look for the physiological correlate which underlies the spatial difference in pitch. The fact that on any place-theory of hearing the lowest tones would fall at the apex and the highest tones at the base of the cochlea opposite the oval window no more means, of course, that we hear the world upside down than that the inversion of the retinal image forces us to stand on our heads to see the world right side up.[22] The experiments were done, however, not so much with auditory theory in mind as with the query as to whether the results would throw any light on the moot question of the apparent movement which most people profess to find in auditory

[22] One observer stood on his head and found that the direction of high and low tones then seemed reversed.

materials as used in musical design. This question will occupy us later. For the present it is enough to point out that in addition to the purely qualitative pitch-character by which tones are readily placed with respect to each other along a scale there may be discovered an intrinsic spatial character in tones which makes it unnecessary to draw upon association to account for the universality of the words "high" and "low."

8. *Volume*

In addition to the dimension of pitch, tones also possess a dimension which can only be described as massiveness or voluminousness. Although this dimension may have some very obscure relation to visual space, and certainly may be reinforced by associations with space, it must nevertheless be insisted that as given directly in auditory experience under ideal conditions of observation the volumic property of tones is sensed as something distinctly different from spatial extent. The bigness or smallness of tones cannot be estimated in terms of centimeters. Careful observers, however, find it quite possible to estimate the volume of one tone in relation to the volume of another, and these observations indicate conclusively that volume decreases progressively from the lowest to the highest tones.[23] Volume must therefore (on the physical side) be a function of vibration-frequency, but the function is mathematically different from that for pitch since the latter follows an arithmetical progression, whereas volume appears to have a geometrical relation to frequency, which means that discriminations of pitch are much finer than those of volume. Since musical intervals also bear a geometrical relation to frequency, it has been suggested that the dimension of volume is basic to the perception of interval.[24] At all events, the sense of pitch is certainly not crucial to the perception of intervals, for several pitches may be transversed before a tone is recognized as having moved by as much as a semitone.

9. *Timbre*

Only by means of very special apparatus is it possible to set up *simple* periodic vibrations. All musical instruments produce periodic vibrations, but the forms of the waves are complex, and these various complexities of wave-form are the physical correlates of the tonal properties which the musi-

[23] G. J. Rich, "A Study of Tonal Attributes," *American Journal of Psychology*, 1919, 30, 121–164.
[24] R. M. Ogden, *Hearing*, 66–69, 121–123.

cian calls *quality* or *tone-color*, and the psychologist calls *timbre*. It is by these properties that the distinctive qualities of the different musical instruments are so readily identified by the practiced ear. A moment's reflection makes it clear that timbre must be independent of pitch, for the same pitch may be sounded by different instruments, but the qualities of the tones produced by these several instruments are all markedly dissimilar.

The physical explanation of timbre appears simple enough. By a mathematical principle known as Fourier's theorem it can be demonstrated that all complex periodic wave-forms are reducible to a system of superimposed simple partial vibrations whose frequencies are multiples of the frequency of the fundamental. A string, for example, vibrates not only as a whole (first partial or fundamental), but also in halves (second partial), thirds, quarters, *etc*. Further investigation has demonstrated that the differences in wave-forms of different instruments reside chiefly in the number and relative intensities of the component partials. The oboe, for example, has twelve partials, with the fourth and fifth partials much more intense than the others, while the clarinet has nearer twenty partials, with the eighth, ninth, and tenth predominating.

At the risk of too frequent digression, it would be well at this point to emphasize again the difference between an *explanation*, such as the one in the preceding paragraph, and a *description*, and to illustrate the difference by the concrete fact of timbre; for a consideration of the difference between an explanation and a description of timbre will serve to illustrate the kind of confusion which, at a higher level, has been responsible for a great deal of misunderstanding in musical aesthetics. If the reader will keep in mind certain of the consequences which follow from a consideration of this concrete example, he will appreciate more readily the problems to be treated in later sections.

Timbre defies good description. A person may identify the experience easily enough, and may assign a word to it or accept whatever word may happen to exist for the particular experience, but if he is to do more than point to the experience by means of a word-symbol, he will find himself floundering about in a welter of words all of which will strike him as pitifully inadequate as conveyors of the unique *quale* of the experience. Consider the tone of an oboe. In the last analysis, the quality of tone from an oboe can only be described in terms of itself, for, to define the true quality of an oboe-tone, what is it but to be nothing else but the quality of tone from an oboe? More or less feeble efforts may be made to characterize the quality further by observing that there is something rough, raspy, nasal, penetrating, thin, pungent, mordant, or sharp about it, but these words are all immediately recognized as deficient. So much for description. How about explaining the tone of an oboe? An explanation of the oboe-tone will involve an enumeration of the *conditions* which underlie the production of the tone.

In our present state of knowledge the most accessible of these conditions happen to be those found in the wave-form produced by the instrument itself—the partials mentioned above. By a little training, however, it is possible for a person actually to hear, in listening to an oboe, some of these partials, or rather, the phenomenal tones correlated with these partials. This fact has led many psychologists to explain timbre as an integration of overtones intimately fused. "Psychologically, timbre is to be understood and explained as a complex of pitches fused into a single tone."[25] "The timbre of the compound tone is, in the main, the unanalysed resultant of the tone-colours of its simple constituents."[26] "The peculiar and characteristic sound of a given musical instrument is due to the fusion of tones of fixed pitch-relations."[27] This type of explanation must be flatly rejected as in-

[25] C. E. SEASHORE, *Introduction to Psychology*, 1923, 62.
[26] E. B. TITCHENER, *Text-book of Psychology*, 102.
[27] M. BENTLEY, *The Field of Psychology*, 123.

correct on the grounds of the inescapable fact that psychologically the tone from an oboe simply is *not* the fusion or resultant of simpler constituents.

In hearing the oboe one is ordinarily not in the least aware of a multiplicity of tones, but only of a single tone. It is probably safe to hazard the guess that ninety-nine out of every one hundred oboe-players never heard the overtones of their own instruments, and yet every last player would be sensitive to the quality of the tone and to differences in quality brought about by poor reeds, bad lip, temperature, *etc*. Now if a tone can be immediately identified as that of an oboe without any awareness whatsoever of overtones, then it must follow that *psychologically* the tone is not the sum or integration of a fundamental and its overtones, for the simple reason that the quality of the tone can exist perfectly well *without* the awareness of the overtones. But what about the overtones which can be heard after a little practice? Must they not really be there all the time even when one fails to hear them? If the second question has any meaning at all it surely must be answered flatly in the negative. In order for an overtone to exist psychologically someone must hear it, so that the question should read, Are not these overtones really being heard all the time even when one fails to hear them?

The proper interpretation of the overtones which can be analysed out of an oboe-tone has already been mentioned under the phrase *physiological determination*. Since under identical conditions of stimulation various overtones may be revealed at the level of consciousness at different moments of observation, the reasonable view would seem to be that these overtones are the reflections in consciousness of the physiological processes which lie in the region of direct determination and are immediately responsible for the peculiar quality of the oboe. Just as the physician regards the aches and pains reported by his patient as symptoms of underlying physiological disturbances, so the psychologist reads the introspective reports of his trained observers as accounts which furnish clues to the nature of the physiological processes which determine the experiences mentioned in the reports. Since these processes are complex in composition there are various *potential* correlates in consciousness, although at any one moment the actual correlates may be reduced to a single item of experience. Three corollaries or consequences of this view should be noted and borne in mind during the later discussions of music. To mention these consequences would be platitudinous were it not for the fact that they are so flagrantly disregarded in theories of music.

a. No psychological experience can be identified with the conditions enumerated in its explanation. Most of the conditions of experience exist in the physiological processes of the organism and in the physical aspects of the stimulus, but in neither of these domains are the psychological properties of experience to be found.

b. Even when the conditions include psychological processes, these processes can not be substituted for the original experience itself. They are among the conditions of the experience, but are not identical with it.

c. Psychological processes which are only discovered after minute analysis are not to be regarded as meanings, in the sense in which the term is here used, in spite of the fact that the observation of these processes is a matter of learning. Learning and meaning are not synonymous, as is often assumed to be the case on the basis of uncritical acceptance of the idea that all meaning is a product of past experience. To hear overtones in an oboe requires learning and practice, and the great majority of mankind go through life without ever having heard them, but this fact should not be taken as evidence that when a person has discovered overtones he has enriched his experience with a new meaning, for these overtones sustain a definite functional relationship to the stimulus, and are no more meanings than the oboe-tone itself.

10. *Auflösungsbedürfniss*

Other attributive aspects of tones, such as *vowel-quality* and *brightness*, have received considerable attention at the hands of psychologists, and many technical problems relating to them, as well as to the attributes already mentioned, are badly in need of further investigation. Their solution is more important, however, for auditory theory than for the special problems of music. Enough has already been said to make clear what auditory experiences may be designated as the *materials* of music. Nor is it necessary to do more than mention in passing those sensory attributes, such as *intensity* and *duration*, which are common to all sense departments. Their rôle in music is of the utmost significance and will be commented upon later. In the present context it is sufficient to remember that when perceived as the properties of tones they are to be included among the materials of music. A tone of given pitch may be loud or soft, long or short. It is these variations, in all their richness of gradation, which are comprehended under the terms intensity and duration.

One characteristic of tones not yet mentioned has frequently puzzled psychologists with respect to its proper classification. Brief consideration of this particular difficulty, although of no immediate concern to music, will serve to single out precisely the sort of problem which not infrequently leads to confusion in discussions of music. If one listens to an ascending scale of notes moving through a range of several octaves and keeps the first note especially in mind, he will observe that at stated intervals a tone appears which bears a striking resemblance to the first note of the series. If, for example, the series begins on *c*, all subsequent *c*'s sound alike, although no two have the same pitch. If some other tone is kept in mind, the same resemblance of certain of the tones will be discovered. All tones, in fact, which bear an octave-relation to each other reveal a qualitative similarity (their *c*-ness, *f*-ness, *d*-sharp-ness, *b*-flat-ness, *etc.*), as well as a pitch-difference. It is this repetition of qualitative likeness throughout the tonal continuum which goes by the name of *octave-quality* or, in many psychological texts, *tonality*. The question immediately arises for psychology: Is tonality a simple tonal attribute, the property of a single tone? Although it is not impossible to find tonality listed among the simple tonal attributes,[28]

[28] E. B. TITCHENER, *A Beginner's Psychology*, 52. In his *Text-book* Titchener treats of tonality under perceptual experience. This difference in the two books may reflect his own uncertainty as to the proper classification of tonality.

the more frequent argument maintains that inasmuch as the similarity which confers upon two tones an octave-quality in common can not have arisen except by one tone having been perceived in relation to another, tonality must be regarded not as a simple auditory attribute, but as an attribute of a higher order, an attribute of tonal form. "We may for the present pass over the octave-quality as an elemental attribute of tone, our cursory examination having shown us that the octave always implies at least two tones in a perceptive configuration . . . Taken strictly by itself, a simple tone does not seem to warrant an inference regarding its octave, or regarding any other musical relationship."[29]

If in order to be a simple elemental attribute of tone a quality must be inherent in a single item completely isolated from all other auditory experience, it would then follow that practically all so-called simple attributes are not, strictly speaking, simple at all. Ogden's position with respect to the complex nature of the octave-quality is, of course, a perfectly sound one. His argument could be applied equally well, however, to *pitch* and *intensity*. A tone can be recognized as high or low only by virtue of the fact that it has been perceived in relation to other pitches. And the judgment that a

[29] R. M. Ogden, *Hearing*, 55.

tone is loud or soft arises by the same sort of process of comparison. Once these relations have been noted and to some degree systematized the single tones thereafter may be placed with more or less accuracy along their respective dimensions of pitch and intensity. A property which first became palpable in a relationship appears by itself when either of the terms of the relationship is given subsequently in isolation. Considered from this angle it will be seen that the criterion with which Ogden cuts tonality off from the simple attributes is capable, if applied sharply, of hewing away everything except bare sound itself. The status thus conferred upon the so-called simple attributes does not concern the present discussion. The supposed implications of the same line of argument, when turned in the direction of the complex attributes, do concern the present discussion very directly.

Tonality, or octave-quality, is only one among numerous qualities which may come into existence when two or more tones are observed in a relationship. Tonality, to be sure, occupies a somewhat unique position inasmuch as the terms in the relation bear a striking resemblance to each other. Many other tonal relationships, however, are fully as real psychologically and just as easily identified by anyone who has occasion to note them. Tonality,

on the side of stimulus, is conditioned by frequencies which stand in the ratio of 1:2. How
about the ratios 2:3, 4:5, 3:5, and 9:16? Are the
interval-qualities of the fifth, the major third, the
major sixth, and the minor seventh any less
dependent on tones perceived in a relationship
than is the octave-quality? In the latter case,
either note of the octave, when presented singly
and listened to under the proper attitude, seems
partially to possess, or partake of, the quality of
the other. Only to a somewhat less extent is this
also true of the single components of other interval-
relationships. All the notes in a melodic sequence,
for example, bear to each other a definite relation
determined by the key in which the melody is
written, and these relations are often apparent
even when certain of the terms needed to complete
the relation are not actually given. If a very simple
melody is written in the key of *D* and the next to
last note falls on *e*, an interruption of the melody
at that point will make it almost painfully apparent
that the note *e* has already entered into and
acquired the characteristics of a very specific tonal
relationship. The character which *e* now reveals
is determined by the physical ratio 8:9 (occasionally 3:4) fixed by the tonal progressions in the key
of *D*. How different this *e* would have sounded had
the key been four sharps! In two sharps its charac-

ter can fittingly be described as a *need for resolution*. Appropriate harmonization may greatly enhance this same character.

In this character of suspense, or need for resolution, the musician will recognize at once a familiar example of innumerable effects created by the intricate network of melodic, contrapuntal, and harmonic relationships through which tonal material weaves its way. Are these effects to be regarded, psychologically, as meanings? The question is important, for the interpretation of many problems in aesthetic theory is influenced by the answer.

One simple way of coming to a decision in this question would be to reason that since these effects do not differ from octave-quality in kind but merely in degree of complexity, whatever classification is accorded the former should, by the same token, be assigned to the latter. Although, as we have already seen, octave-quality is not generally regarded as a simple auditory attribute, it is certainly quite universally considered to be, at all events, an attribute of a higher order—a quality inherent in the formal structure of tonal combination. No one has ever maintained, as far as I know, that octave-quality is a contextual supplementation having its source in processes extraneous to the auditory material itself. From this it would seem to be permissible to conclude that all musical effects due intrinsically to the relations between the tones themselves are formal, not meaningful attributes.

Another way of arriving at the same conclusion follows from the more restricted sense in which the concept of meaning is here being applied. Instead of spreading the concept indiscriminately over nearly the whole field of phenomenal experience, the position is here taken that only those events deserve strictly to be labelled meanings which disclose no dependency upon the physical constitution of the stimulus. As far back as the time of the Pythagoreans it was discovered that many musical relationships could be interpreted functionally in terms of simple ratios between lengths of strings and pipes, while today it is theoretically possible to write a mathematical formula which will satisfy a whole musical composition. Such a task has never, of course, been actually undertaken, but the possibility of doing so nevertheless remains.

In the case of the unresolved cadence mentioned above, the relation to the stimulus is direct and unequivocal. If the *e* descends a whole tone to *d* the need for resolution is adequately met, and the interval which satisfies this need corresponds to the stimulus ratio 8:9. Any slight departure from this ratio or the substitution of another one (3:4, ascending fourth to *a*) destroys the resolution completely or introduces one of an entirely different character. Such close dependency upon the physical properties of the stimulus makes it impossible to regard these and similar musical effects as meanings. That they may invite contextual supplementation from various extraneous sources by way of the ordinary channels of association and thus produce phenomena which are to be indubitably classed as meanings is not for a moment denied. The tonic resolution of a cadence may seem to speak, in the minds of some listeners, of the final peace which follows a life of virtuous struggle. Such an interpretation, however, is totally irrelevant and unessential to the existence and appearance of the musical quality of resolution as such.

The besetting sin of certain schools of psychology has been the use of the concept "meaning" as a sort of wastebasket into which could be thrown various psychological experiences which did not yield conveniently to description in terms of simple sensory process. A procedure similar in many ways is frequently resorted to by writers on music who, obsessed by the notion that all varieties of formalism are inimical to the highest interests of musical theory, refuse to include within the formal structure of music the type of impression produced by a falling cadence. Relief from suspense, or the continuation of suspense when a melody ends on the fifth of the scale—these, the expressionist would argue, are meanings which have accrued to the purely auditory core of the music, and, as such, must be numbered among the characteristics of musical expression rather than musical form. If, however, it can be argued with some show of reason that these impressions may be interpreted as the intrinsic property of musical form, not only will much confusion be saved by placing them where they rightly belong, but by thus invoking the scientific law of parsimony a simpler explanation of their occurrence will be found. Meaning and expression present a much more baffling problem to psychology than do perception and form. Any legitimate diminution of the former and expansion of the latter is therefore obviously desirable.

Already the problem of musical form has made its appearance. Tonality, or octave-quality, if shown to be the property of two tones in a perceptive configuration, belongs strictly in the domain of form rather than material. The very difficulty, however, which psychology has had with octave-quality only demonstrates the folly of attempting to separate material and form too rigidly. There can be no form which is not the form of some material, and in music, certainly, there can be no material which is not presented in one form or another, however simple and rudimentary. But by however much separation makes for artificial abstraction, by just so much is it necessary to introduce artificiality into the critical analysis of a living pleasurable experience like music.

11. *The Importance of Material in Music*

The conditions which make for pleasure in an object of art are too numerous and complicated to permit of any dogmatic estimate regarding their relative importance, unless by "conditions" one means the gross divisions of the aesthetic experience itself into material, form, and meaning—in which case the generalization that form is the most potent factor, for certain arts at all events, would seem to be reasonably safe. The great significance of form often tends, however, to obscure the pervasive rôle of material. And the silly conceit that the sensuous stuff of experience is lowly and base undoubtedly brings it about in many cases that the senses actually become sluggish to the charms which lie in this direction.

The first task of the artist must always be to discover the sensuous medium most suitable to convey to others the emotions and ideas which seize upon his imagination, no matter how lofty and sublime and removed from palpable reality the contents of his imagination may be. The sensuous medium is no less potential for aesthetic pleasure when its very inadequacy for portraying the sublime becomes the means by which the mind is carried beyond the limitations of direct perception. Yet not all forms of art share equally the benefits of sensuous material. A crude illustration of this difference may serve to clarify the rôle of material in music as compared with the material, for example, of poetry.

The natural approach to words is non-aesthetic. The primary function of language centers about the communication of ideas and thoughts, and the relation between these meanings and the sound of their verbal symbols has long since been lost sight of, except in the case of onomatopoesis. If the reader will make note of the first words which come into his mind when he is presented with simple words like *table*, *sun*, and *dog*, he will undoubtedly find himself thinking of words like *chair*, *moon*, and *cat*. That is to say, word-associations come almost invariably by way of meanings or logical relationships. Only in rare instances would a person think of *label*, *pun*, and *log*, or other associations determined by the sound of the words. And yet these latter words are all associations by similarity, and similarity is one of the main grooves through which associations run. Similarity of sound, however, recedes to the dim margins of consciousness in ordinary verbal discourse in order to leave room in the focus of attention for the more important task of understanding and following the logical interrelations of meanings. Such preoccupation with the meaning to the exclusion of the sound of words is definitely inimical to full aesthetic enjoyment, for it is characteristic of the genuine aesthetic attitude to linger expectantly at the threshold and surface of experience in order to savor whatever of sensuous loveliness the artist has placed there. If the artist moulds his object out of words he must exercise his skill with a material which in the minds of many people stubbornly refuses to put off its prosaic habit of serving merely as a guide in directing the traffic of practical behavior. Even for lovers of poetry who have become keenly sensitive to nuances of verbal sound 't is questionable whether the purely auditory aspects of the most exquisitely chosen words ever secure coercive power for attention comparable to that of musical sounds.

For those with ears to hear, poetry does possess, of course, its own unique share of auditory sensuous material. Those who doubt this fact would do well to listen attentively to great poetry spoken in a language totally unfamiliar to them. In such an experience the careful thought which the poet has given to the sound of the words becomes apparent at once. In one's own mother tongue, however, no such complete divorce of sound and meaning is likely to be achieved under ordinary conditions of listening or reading. And even if it were, the dimensions of verbal sound would still be far more restricted than those of musical sound.

Failure to be moved with concord of sweet sounds, if not high moral treason, is most certainly a sign that the motions of the musical spirit are dull. The very protoplasm of such enjoyment begins to disintegrate whenever the quality of tone ceases to be important. The formal outline of a Bach fugue remains the same whether it be played on a one-manual reed organ in the village church or on the finest creation of Cavaillé-Coll. But if after hearing both kinds of organ, it is still a matter of indifference to the lover of Bach upon which set of diapasons his fugues are sounded forth, then, truly, a lamentable fate has overtaken his musical appreciation. Only those who are old in the art of listening, whose memories are filled to overflowing with the perfections of sound, can afford to rest content with the subtler satisfactions to be derived from the perception of formal musical relationships. For less experienced listeners it is a healthy sign when the utmost excellence of tonal production is demanded, when virtuosity is valued above intelligence of musical performance. In those whose interest in music is genuine such demands and preferences are sure indication that the ear is caught by the fanfare and flourish of sound for its own sake. A wise teacher of music will not be discouraged by the boy who prefers the saxaphone to the viola or Gershwin to Händel.

When people show themselves indifferent to primary and fundamental effects, when they are incapable of finding pictures except in frames or beauties except in the great masters, we may justly suspect that they are parrots, and that their verbal and historical knowledge covers a natural lack of aesthetic sense. Where, on the contrary, insensibility to higher forms of beauty does not exclude a natural love of the lower, we have every reason to be encouraged; there is a true and healthy taste, which only needs experience to refine it. If a man demands light, sound, and splendour, he proves that he has the aesthetic equilibrium; that appearances as such interest him, and that he can pause in perception to enjoy. We have but to vary his observation, to enlarge his thought, to multiply his discriminations—all of which education can do—and the same aesthetic habit will reveal to him every shade of the fit and fair. Or if it should not, and the man, although sensuously gifted, proved to be imaginatively dull, at least he would not have failed to catch an intimate and widespread element of effect. The beauty of material is thus the groundwork of all higher beauty, both in the object, whose form and meaning have to be lodged in something sensible, and in the mind, where sensuous ideas, being the first to emerge, are the first that can arouse delight.[30]

[30] G. SANTAYANA, *op. cit.*, 80*f.*

Part II

The Form of Music

1. *The Importance of Form in Art*

In its very broadest sense form may be taken to include all the divers ways in which the sensuous materials of experience are moulded and patterned at the hand of the artist. Since for all practical purposes of artistic technique the possible permutations and combinations of sensuous material are well nigh inexhaustible and since the likelihood of exact duplication among these combinations is about as great as would be the appearance in nature of two trees identical in outline, the enumeration of the varieties of formal structure would be tantamount to listing every object of art which had ever been created. Each work of art is in possession of unique formal properties. And yet in spite of this extreme individuation it becomes apparent even upon superficial examination that most variations in form may be subsumed under a relatively small number of types.

The exact number and characteristics of these types of formal structure have been the subject of interminable discussions on the part of aestheticians and critics for over two thousand years. Aesthetic theory began, as a matter of fact, by raising the problem of form, and the subsequent tenacity of formalistic aesthetics is in itself an interesting question to those concerned with the history of aesthetic theory. By most Greek thinkers the work of the artist was regarded as a semblance or appearance of reality, subject to the same standards of criticism and investigation as reality itself. This metaphysical principle, with its moralistic corollary, affords a partial explanation of the preponderance of abstract formalism in those portions of Greek philosophy which deal directly with the problem of aesthetic value; for if the beauty of art can lay claim to no qualities or attributes other than those already revealed in nature, can shadow forth no regions in which the human spirit transcends nature, then an explanation of beauty is sufficiently given in terms of certain abstract principles by the exercise of which the representation of nature is most successfully accomplished. Foremost among these principles was that of unity in variety—a principle which has remained the point of departure for formalism ever since Hellenic antiquity.

It is worthy of note that in a subject like aesthetics, where opinion far outruns fact, there is to be found at least one principle upon which all writers agree, no matter whether their temperament inclines them in the direction of the far-flung speculations of Plato or the minute experimental researches of Fechner. The importance of form in general may be variously estimated. Never is it treated, however, as completely irrelevant, and its most striking and frequent mode of appearance is unfailingly seen to be by way of unity in variety, harmony, coherence, proportion, symmetry, the subtler balance of asymmetrical distributions, consonance, organic continuity, concordant relation of parts, homogeneity—the terminology is not always the same, but the underlying principle remains largely unaltered.

Much of the dispute over the interpretation of the principle revolves about the very natural question as to the extent to which it may legitimately be applied. Here again, unanimity of opinion is greater than one might expect. New art-forms frequently embarrass aesthetic theory by giving rise to a general impression that the old rules have now been thrown into the discard. This view is strengthened both by the radicals in art who loudly proclaim the dawn of a new era and by the conservatives who bitterly lament the passing of the golden age. Those who were young when Wagner's *Tristan* first made its appearance were sure that they would never hear the like again until they reached heaven, while those who were old were equally certain that a second hearing of it would kill them. One has only to listen to the comments after a concert of modern music today to discover that the history of art is still repeating itself.

With the passage of time, however, those new forms of art which succeed in giving pleasure to an ever-increasing number of people invariably turn out to be the ones in which an inner logicality, at first concealed by unfamiliarity, may be discovered. Although the arrangement of parts may be very complex, often anomalous and even bizarre, certainly novel and unfamiliar, yet they are held together by some principle of coherence, so that the inclusion of such forms under a principle of organic unity is very generally regarded as a justifiable extension of ancient aesthetic doctrine. The increase in complexity of structure by no means precludes the operation of a unifying factor, although this factor may not be apparent at first sight. The principle of selection in the following two series of numbers is seen at a glance in *A*, whereas in *B* it is not nearly so obvious.

A	2	4	6	8	10	12	14	16	18	20	22	24	26
B	1	7	2	6	4	10	5	9	7	13	8	12	10

Now in *B* the selection was certainly not a random or haphazard one for the person who chose the numbers. For the person who looks at them for the first time, however, the choice may seem perfectly arbitrary and formless. For him, *B*, psychologically, simply does not have a unifying principle. From the assertion that *B* is an example of a series of numbers whose relations to one another possess a certain inner logicality he would dissent most emphatically on the basis of what is to him quite truly a self-evident proposition that it does *not* possess this vaunted logicality. Of an exactly comparable nature, alas, are many of the bitter quarrels over the relative merits of different works of art! Substitute for *A* a minuet by Haydn and for *B* a ballet by Strawinsky, and the analogy becomes clear enough.

Not all *apparent* increases in complexity should be considered as real. Complexity is endowed with a very subtle sort of psychological relativity. Exactly the same stimulus may yield, at different times, two very different kinds of experience, one simple and the other complex, but both identified as coming from the same physical object. A group of black dots on a cardboard, for example, may be perceived simply as a mass of dots too numerous, in a short exposure, to be counted, and therefore a bit confusing. The impression is judged as complex. At another exposure, however, the same dots may be seen to have a fairly simple geometrical design. The design, as such, now occupies the center of attention and the separate dots, by snapping into their proper positions within the design, recede to the margin of attention. The impression is judged as simple. Which is it, really,—simple or complex? It all depends upon what one means by "really." *Psychologically* the impression is whatever it is judged to be. No science or logic in the world can defend the position that a person's experience is anything different from what he says it is. If, however, one refers to the dots on the card as something independent of one's experience of it, then, strictly speaking, this something is neither simple nor complex, for simplicity and complexity, in the present context, are properties relative to human perception. All of us have the inveterate habit, however, of regarding our impressions as enjoying an existence quite apart from our awareness of them, and of ascribing to these independently-existing objects the *same* properties which we find directly in our impressions. In the course of time, therefore, our idea of the permanent possibilities of an object assumes the character of a composite abstraction made up of those impressions which have gained ascendancy through primacy, recency, frequency, vividness, interest, or what not. If our impressions undergo a change we are likely to speak as though the object itself had changed, and we find ourselves insisting that what seemed originally complex is *really* after all quite simple. The epistemological ambiguity involved in such a statement ordinarily occasions no confusion. In certain instances, however, it is well at least to be aware of the existence of the ambiguity. Such instances frequently occur in judgments regarding the complexity of a work of art.

If complexity has any meaning apart from its application to the character of a psychological impression, it would seem that it can only refer to the actual number of physical variables of an object or to their mode of interrelation. Thus defined, it by no means follows that the more complex *psychological* impression is correlated with the more complex *physical* stimulus. It may very well happen that the simpler of two physical objects is perceived in such a way that the parts of the perception do not hang together at all, whereas the more complex physical object may give rise to an impression amazingly simple. Many baffling and confusing modern compositions are almost stupidly simple in their underlying physical structure. Many Bach fugues, on the other hand, would present a terrifying task to the person who wished to analyse the mathematical ratios of the notes, and yet they would be judged by most musicians to be without parallel in music with respect to their directness, simplicity, and coherence of structure.

Whatever ambiguity attaches to the use of the concept of complexity, it nevertheless remains theoretically possible to consider the underlying physical properties of works of art as susceptible of alignment into a continuum of complexity, ranging all the way from the very simplest to the most complex, and to assume, furthermore, that before organization into forms and patterns has been realized there would tend to be a positive correlation between this continuum and the continuum of impressions ordered according to *psychological* complexity. By the time, however, that repetition of the same stimuli has afforded opportunity for the discovery of various internal relations, the order of impressions will be very considerably altered.

Beyond any question of doubt the most significant factors in bringing about the realignment of impressions are those which have to do with the shaping of new unities in the multiplicities of materials. In our present state of knowledge regarding these factors it would be a rash person indeed who would dare hazard a guess as to how far an artist may go in his manipulation of subtle internal relations before he reaches what may be termed the upper threshold of unity in variety. The mind reveals a truly extraordinary ability to subordinate wealth of parts in favor of singleness of general outline, and no one can as yet foresee the limits of the mind's capacity in this direction. But no matter what degree of plasticity may be shown in this respect, it is a reasonably safe assumption that the principles of mental organization will everywhere turn out to be closely related—will, as a matter of fact, be variations in the manifestation of a single psychophysiological mechanism.

The reasons for the important rôle of formal structure in art must be sought, along with the reasons for whatever other relevant factors may ever be discovered, in the domain of psychological affectivity, *i.e.*, in the pleasure which the individual derives from the contemplation of these factors. What the nature of the underlying psychophysiological mechanism of formal structure may be and *why* the operation of this mechanism is accompanied by pleasure are problems still shrouded in obscurity. Various lines of evidence point to a close affinity between certain aesthetic principles and the general biological principle of equilibrium. Between every organism and its environment there exists a certain set of conditions which must be maintained within well-defined limits if the processes of life are to continue. The optimum temperature of the medium for *Paramecium aurelia*, for example, ranges from 24 to 28 degrees. Any departure from this range initiates movements on the part of the animal which continue until equilibrium is restored.

This principle of equilibrium has obvious applications, as an hypothesis, to the complex ramifications of human mental life. With a view to securing for himself as much pleasure and satisfaction out of life as possible a man formulates an elaborate plan of action the complete details of which will not be realized for a number of years. For such an individual psychological equilibrium is maintained only when the number of conditions which favor his life-plan are in excess of those which upset it. Those events which further the plan bring pleasure; those which hinder it result in unhappiness.

Just so in writing a composition of music, the composer conceives his kaleidoscope of sensuous materials in terms of a total plan or structure. That the degree to which the listener apprehends this structure is directly proportional to the pleasure which he takes in the composition is a hypothesis already grounded in considerable empirical observation. In terms of this hypothesis the wide individual variations characteristic of the apprehension of musical form would serve partially to account for the great differences in affective value which different people attach to the same composition. The person who professes to find nothing but superficial gayety in Mozartean music simply does not move in the same auditory world with him who discovers in Mozart a measured melancholy which, under the baton of a conductor like Dr. Muck, may be sharpened for brief moments to the point of exquisite pain.

A lengthier consideration of such a hypothesis is not to the purpose in the present context. Enough has been said to emphasize the general agreement regarding the importance of form in the aesthetic experience. The very importance of form, however, demands a digression at this point.

2. *No Single Criterion of Aesthetic Value*

Ever since earliest times writers on the subject of aesthetics have tried to find a single and unique factor which would distinguish the aesthetic experience from all other possible experiences. Unfortunately, the number of factors which have been proposed is rather considerable, and the roads along which the traffic of aesthetic theory has passed during its history are littered with the débris of mighty and valiant combats waged over this one question. And as yet there are no signs that the excitement is abating, for during the last three years at least three important contributions to aesthetics have appeared, in each one of which a different position regarding the ultimate nature of the aesthetic experience has been defended.[1]

The troublesome fact with which aestheticians have had to contend whenever they have set out to define art in terms of a single criterion has been the obstinate refusal of aesthetic experience to submit to any such strait-jacket. For every criterion proposed a list of exceptions can be read off, and the defenders of the respective criteria either attempt desperately to explain the exceptions away or pass over them in silence. One would suppose that after this process of selection and exclusion had gone to the point of exhausting practically all available criteria without arriving at any satisfactory conclusion, aestheticians would take seriously the problem of discovering, if possible, the source of the trouble. Students of aesthetics, however, seem to glory in violent conflict of opinion— as though any real resolution of a disagreement would result in stagnation.

A review of the long line of answers, with their arguments, which have been given to the question "What is art?" might possibly be amusing—but

[1] D. H. PARKER, *The Analysis of Art*, 1926; D. W. PRALL, *Aesthetic Judgment*, 1929; and C. J. DUCASSE, *The Philosophy of Art*, 1929.

it would more likely be tedious and unprofitable. A brief indication of the difficulty in formulating an answer must be sufficient. As has already been stated, the Greeks tended to regard art as an imitation of reality and drew the corollary that the peculiar power of art must be sought in certain abstract principles of form. In many types of art it is plainly true that an appearance or semblance of reality exists, and the only successful denial of this fact by those who have no use whatever for this view is accomplished by the convenient method of refusing to recognize this type of art as legitimate. The weakness of the imitation-theory as a general principle is, however, only too obvious today, as are also the weaknesses of views which emphasize factors of utility, commemoration, decoration, ornamentation, *etc.*

The corollary of Greek theory regarding form, on the other hand, has maintained a prominent place wherever questions of art have received serious consideration. One factor which lends great strength to the position of the formalist has frequently been overlooked, even by those most outspoken in their defense of form. Some of the conditions which underlie the perception of form reside within the object itself. To the extent, therefore, to which form plays a rôle in the aesthetic experience it can be demonstrated that that portion of the experience (plus all the sensuous content) depends largely upon what the artist has done with his materials rather than upon the imaginative and associative supplementation of the person who beholds his work. The value of the experience has its permanent residence in the work of art itself, and although the experiential correlate of this work is subject to no little variation, its stability and likelihood of recurrence are far, far greater than can possibly be the case with those experiences richly filled out with associated and extraneous meanings and imaginings. These latter come and go, change and decay, whereas the former are always potentially there and may be turned to again and again for renewed delight. It is small wonder that many teachers of music deplore the use of stories as an aid in listening to music. The music itself is the thing!

Part of the purpose of the present volume is to suggest that the degree to which formal structure may be drawn upon to account for the power of music has not been fully realized even by the formalists themselves. It must not be understood, however, that this attempt still further to enlarge the rôle assigned to form carries with it any implication that form precludes the operation of other factors. Such a view would be fully as untenable as any of those which seek for a single criterion of art.

One may feel himself tempted, particularly in music, to rank form first among several factors. "Nevertheless, the conclusion of the formalist that aesthetic form is all there is to beauty is unfounded."[2] But it is equally true that the conclusion of any writer on aesthetics that some other one factor is all there is to beauty is also unfounded.

Types of aesthetic theory which differ most radically from ancient doctrine are likely to center about the contention that art is symbolic, that the object given to perception is interpenetrated with meanings for which the bare perceptual qualities serve merely as a sign or symbol. These views derive largely from the Hegelian doctrine of idealization and contain, from whatever psychological angle one regards them, a profound and undeniable truth. Again, however, it is a question of how exclusively this symbolic factor operates.

The assertion . . . that in aesthetic perception what is given is an object interpenetrated with meanings and a sense of tendencies brought to fruition, seems to me very questionable. The most that could be said, I think, is that that is *sometimes* the case . . . In the aesthetic perception of colors and tones as such, for instance, no interpenetrating meaning or sense of tendencies brought to fruition need in the least be involved; nor, in my own case, is it involved in numerous instances of the aesthetic perception even of facts

[2] D. H. PARKER, *op. cit.*, 32.

into which it might more easily be imported,—rainbows, sunsets, the colors and patterns of flowers, fabrics, *etc.* . . . Meaning within the object of aesthetic perception is possible, but not at all necessary.[3]

A newer tendency in aesthetic theory, exemplified in the works of Parker and Ducasse, places greater emphasis on the affective and conative sides of mental life. With uncommon sensitiveness to subtle psychological distinctions Parker persuades his reader to entertain the suggestion that art is uniquely defined as the imaginative expression of a wish. No one who is in any sense alive to aesthetic appreciation can fail to be impressed by the weight of conviction which this suggestion seems to carry, especially when thought of in connection with poetry, drama, and literature. Although its extension to the more abstract arts calls for greater efforts of illustration and exposition, even here many obscure corners of experience are made luminous by the supposition that they are manifestations of the devious ways in which the mind declines to leave forever undone those things which it ought not to do. That music not infrequently may be interpreted in some such manner will become apparent later. At present it is again unfortunately necessary to insist that however adequate it may be to certain aspects of art, the

[3] C. J. DUCASSE, *op. cit.*, 88*f.*

view that the aesthetic consciousness always assumes the essential character of wish-fulfillment is patently contradicted by many facts, some of which, curiously enough, may be cited from the pages of Parker's own book.

A poem is not only an expression of feeling, it is patterned words; a musical composition is not only an embodiment of mood, it has a very elaborate harmonic and rhythmic structure; a picture or statue is never merely the representation of some object in nature, it is besides a harmony of lines and colors and space elements. A beautiful building is never one that is merely well adapted to its purpose, it possesses besides proportion and expressive lines and space forms. No matter how interesting and noble be the imagination of the artist, without design there is no picture or statue or poem or beautiful building.[4]

At the very outset of his first chapter Parker, in referring to the inability of aestheticians to find a satisfactory theory of art, gives it as his opinion that

. . . the chief reason for their failure is the mistaken faith that some single, simple formula can contain the essence of art, whereas art is a very complex, and also a very special sort of thing, that requires a correspondingly complex formula to do it justice. Most of the statements that men have made about art are true enough, but unfortunately

[4] D. H. PARKER, *op. cit.*, 29.

they are also true of many other things, or else leave out of account aspects of art equally essential.[5]

This opinion is worthy of serious attention, but its author gives it little heed when he proceeds to subsume all aspects of art under the formula of wish-fulfillment.

Much of the fascinating illustrative material which Parker draws upon to prove his thesis relates to the underlying motives of creative activity in art. Here, it is maintained, one discovers the working out of a desire on the part of the artist to give expression in sensuous form to the products of his fertile and vivid imagination. All creative activity, from this point of view, may therefore be regarded as the expression of a wish. However true this thesis may be, it must nevertheless be borne clearly in mind that the creation of a work of art by an artist and the enjoyment of this work by another person are two different things, two very different psychological problems. It by no means follows that whatever is true of one is equally true of the other. Hence Parker's concern to get at the underlying motives of creative activity, pertinent as they may be to that particular problem, is beside the point.

That the enjoyment of art rests to some extent upon the release in imagination of longings which

[5] *Ibid.*, 2.

are only partially satisfied in real life may very well be true, but whether it is true or false cannot be demonstrated by an appeal to the mind of the artist. In the light of Freudian doctrine it is a plausible assumption that the elegance, perfection of detail, and refinement of Mozart's music are to be accounted as the tonal embodiment of an imaginative projection which furnished for Mozart a retreat from all the weary, stale, flat, and unprofitable uses of his world. But that the person who enjoys this music must previously have cried out "O God! God!" in the face of a similar world, or that its enjoyment involves the realization of any wish whatever, is open to grave doubt.

Precisely the same objection applies to certain of the arguments which Ducasse uses in defense of his thesis that art is the expression of feeling. Aesthetic theory has dealt primarily with the experience aroused by the perception of works of art, not with the activity which went into the creation of these works. The activity of the artist, although a very real problem in itself, is a means to an end. The *results* of this activity as given in perception, furnish the data with which the study of aesthetics must begin. That these results or products of creative activity, when viewed by lovers of art, very frequently give rise to qualities which, by an expansion of the strictly psychological meaning of the word, may very properly be described as feelings is a fact which deserves much more consideration than has ever been given it, and aesthetic theory is under obligation to Ducasse for making the elaboration of this fact the chief aim of his book. But by fixing his gaze too intently on the creative activity of the artist, Ducasse, too, introduces evidence which is not strictly relevant to the problem of the aesthetic experience; and in order to abide by the single criterion of feeling he is obliged to divide art into many categories. Thus it appears that art (skilled activity) may be autotelic (skilled play), ectotelic (skilled work), and endotelic (skilled self-objectification); and that endotelic art may be lectical (skilled objectification of meaning), heuretic (skilled objectification of will), and *aesthetic* (skilled objectification of *feeling*); and that the last-named may be either interpretative autogenous or pure decorative.

Efforts to characterize the aesthetic experience not in terms of the properties of the object given in the experience but rather by reference to the attitude which the individual assumes towards the object reveal greater unanimity of opinion. Whereas towards the vast majority of impressions in life one's attitude is that of practical concern for the consequences which they have for action and thought, occasionally this practical concern is relaxed so that the immediate qualities of an impression are actually taken in their own right. Then it is, according to many writers, that the individual, by virtue of his detachment from practical interests and his contemplation of an object for its own sake, assumes more nearly the genuine aesthetic attitude. The danger of applying this rule too rigidly, however, is recognized implicitly in the very concept which perhaps more than any other in recent times has sensitized aestheticians to the nature of the aesthetic attitude, *viz.*, that of "psychical distance." Bullough maintains[6] that the aesthetic attitude involves a certain degree of detachment, but points out how imperceptibly and easily an attitude may move between two extremes of over- and under-distance. Presumably the best aesthetic attitude is somewhere in the middle—but who can mark off the limits of this attitude, or who can even be sure that the extremes take one completely out of aesthetics?

The degree to which aesthetic value is determined by pleasure and the extent to which the aesthetic experience itself is to be identified with pleasure are problems which have occupied philosophers and psychologists for centuries. That the

[6] E. BULLOUGH, "'Psychical Distance' as a Factor in Art and an Aesthetic Principle," *British Journal of Psychology*, 1912, 5, 87–118.

judgment of relative merit among works of art rests, in the last analysis, upon the affective process of pleasantness is a reasonable assumption borne out by a large number of careful observations and will be taken uncritically for granted in the following pages. Not all pleasures, however, are aesthetic, and ever since Plato writers have put themselves to great pains to discover the criterion which marks off aesthetic pleasures from the affective tone which colors the rest of experience. As in the case of other attempts to find single criteria for aesthetic values, so in this particular case also there has been no conspicuous success.

It would appear that aestheticians are stubbornly unwilling to entertain the idea that aesthetic value is perhaps not susceptible of definition in terms of a single criterion. "Art is a very complex, and also a very special sort of thing, that requires a correspondingly complex formula to do it justice." What this complex formula may turn out to be no one is yet in a position to say. Inability to write the formula, however, in no way precludes the possibility of realizing that when it is written it will of necessity be complex and, what anyone interested in art will be much the wiser for speedily recognizing, that the struggle to force art into a verbal strait-jacket is almost certainly doomed to failure.

Attempts to answer the question, What is art, have many points in common with attempts to furnish an answer to the question, What is intelligence. Laymen, as well as psychologists, are likely to be reasonably convinced of the accuracy of their insight into the nature of intelligence, but when they proceed to give utterance to their views on the subject the seeker for information is either discouraged or amused to discover that the only common factor in the various opinions expressed is the utter lack of agreement among them. Not long ago a number of psychologists held a symposium on the topic of intelligence.[7] A perusal of the definitions there offered would lead one to suspect that the occasion was an immoderate return to the literal meaning of symposium. Any opinion regarding the possible nature of intelligence which was not uttered there was in all likelihood not worth mentioning. Signs of order are beginning to appear, however, amid the guesswork and opinion with which the field of intelligence has been strewn. After years of study of the nature of intelligence and cognition and of applying of various mathematical devices to test-results secured from many quarters, the British psychologist, Spearman, has elaborated a theory of intellectual capacities which

[7] "Intelligence and Its Measurement: a Symposium," *Journal of Educational Psychology*, 1921, 12.

at once explains much of the confusion which heretofore prevailed and offers a means of interpreting all sorts of scattered observations and facts.[8]

From Spearman's work it appears that intelligence is neither a single unitary function nor a host of different abilities. It is both. Every cognitive act

. . . can be divided into two independent parts which possess the following momentous properties. The one part has been called the "general factor" and denoted by the letter g; it is so named because, although varying freely from individual to individual, it remains the same for any one individual in respect of all the correlated abilities. The second part has been called the "specific factor" and denoted by the letter s. It not only varies from individual to individual, but even for any one individual from each ability to another.[9]

In other words, intelligence manifests itself in a wide variety of ways, thus making it extremely difficult even by careful observation to detect any common characteristic which runs through all intellectual operations. This difficulty is increased by the fact that the common characteristic (Spearman's "general factor" or g) may almost completely saturate one act and be present only slightly in another.

[8] C. SPEARMAN, *The Abilities of Man*, 1927.
[9] *Ibid.*, 74 *f*.

Although, however, both of these factors occur in every ability, they need not be equally influential in all. On the contrary, the very earliest application of this mathematical theorem to psychological correlations showed that there the g has a much greater relative influence or "weight" in some of the abilities tested than in others. Means were even found of measuring this relative weight.[10]

Cognition is therefore not reasoning, nor sound judgment, nor ability to detect relationships, nor span of attention, nor range of memory, nor ability to generalize, nor yet any one of a multitude of other abilities, but rather a factor which is present to a greater or less extent in every one of these cognitive functions. If intelligence has any meaning at all, then this general factor, or g, surely must be it.

It is more than likely that the nature and conditions of aesthetic experience will not be understood until some method of analysis is employed similar to the one used by Spearman in his study of cognition. Objectified feeling, wish-fulfillment, contemplation of the sensuous surface of objects, objectified pleasure, imitation, idealization, illusion, empathy, detachment, form, intuition, psychical distance, measured emotion. these, among others, may all be factors which at one time or another enter into experiences which by general consent are

[10] *Ibid.*, 75.

regarded as aesthetic, and yet none of them by itself is sufficient to define the essential nature of art. Only an elaborate empirical analysis of a wide range of affective judgments may ever reveal whether a general factor operates throughout the variety of specific aesthetic factors. A beginning has already been made in this direction by Beebe-Center.[11] In a study of affective judgments on olfactory substances he was able, by the use of Spearman's formula, to determine the presence of a general affective factor in his stimuli, the value of this factor in any given stimulus, and the degree to which the judgments of his observers were determined by the affective value of the stimulus.

It might be added that this line of thought suggests a ready means of distinguishing aesthetic affective value from non-aesthetic—affective value being considered aesthetic in proportion as it is general in the sense in which the term is used above. It also suggests a means of distinguishing between the aesthetically sensitive and the aesthetically dull. Given a set of aesthetic objects, *i.e.*, objects to which there have been assigned entirely general affective values in the sense in which the term is used above, the aesthetic sensitivity of an individual to these objects could be considered a function of the correlation between the affective values assigned by him to the objects and their general affective values.[12]

[11] J. G. Beebe-Center, "General Affective Value," *Psychological Review*, 1929, 36, 472–480.

[12] *Ibid.*, 474 *f.*

This digression into the problem of the nature of art was made in order to warn the reader against too ready an acceptance of some specific factor as the single and final criterion of the aesthetic experience. It is convenient, for purposes of critical study, to mark off certain palpable divisions of aesthetic experience (as was done in the first section of this book), but it is not justifiable, in our present state of knowledge, to suppose that any one or all of such possible divisions must be regarded as crucial or basic for setting off from the rest of the total world of experience those experiences connected with the enjoyment of art. The elevation of a specific factor to the important status of a general factor has been the temptation which aestheticians have been unable to resist for generations. Since the number of specific factors in art may be very large, the continuation of such a practice would lead to greater and greater confusion. Better by far to suspend judgment or to turn to other methods of inquiry![13]

[13] That laboratories of psychology have anything valuable to contribute to this problem is seriously doubted by Ducasse (*op. cit.*, 12 *ff.*). It strikes me as unfortunate, in view of the obvious desirability of securing evidence from as many sources as possible, that Ducasse should have taken it upon himself to utter such oracular and derogatory pronouncements concerning the value of experimental

3. *The Problem of Form in Music*

An adequate theory for the richness of musical experience would involve a better understanding, than is at present available, of the links in the chain leading from stimulus to response. Certain of these links and their connections have yielded to investigation and analysis; others, however, are still shrouded in mystery. To the physicist belongs the task of exploring (1) the properties of musical instruments and (2) the propagation through the air of the sound-waves set up by these instruments. The physiologist follows the transformation and

---

psychology. His point is no more reinforced by his citation of trivial and dreary examples of laboratory work than the same procedure would be if turned towards philosophy itself. "And even if prolonged investigation should establish some statistical law, to the effect, perhaps, that about eighty-seven per cent of native-born American males between the ages of twenty and twenty-five prefer a given color under laboratory conditions, what could be done with that? Possibly it might be of some slight use to the manufacturers of wall-papers for love-nests,—brides' tastes being equal!" (p. 14) Surely Ducasse could not have wanted to leave with his readers the impression that he thought statistics stopped with averages, and that preferential judgments constitute the sole data which the laboratory can furnish to psychological aesthetics.

transmission of energy as these sound-waves impinge upon (3) the organ of hearing and excite (4) the auditory receptors, and studies as best he may the nature of afferent nerve (5) excitation and (6) conduction and the processes at (7) the central region of adjustment.

Immediately correlated with (7), so runs present-day psychophysiological hypothesis, are the phenomena of *direct experience*, of which music is a part. This phenomenal field is the starting-point for all scientific inquiry. Many branches of science, however, have long since restricted their phenomenal field to those events (in physics, chiefly the passage of a needle-point over a line) which serve as indicators of those "physical" properties not given directly in experience. To psychology alone, apparently, belonged for generations the task of exploring the phenomenal field in its own right. And today even psychology, in certain quarters, is coming to regard direct experience rather in the light of a means to an end—the end being the nature of underlying physiological process. This shift of emphasis in psychology does not and can not mean, however, that direct experience is ultimately to be abandoned as a subject-matter of scientific investigation, for no matter how remote and abstract the concepts of science may appear, they are nevertheless designed to furnish an account of the world as we perceive it, and as long as part of this world (ideas, thoughts, emotions, aesthetic values, for example) remains unaccounted for, just so long is the work of science incomplete.

The processes which take place in (7) the central region of adjustment pass over at this point from the sensory to the motor areas and give rise to (8) efferent nerve conduction leading to (9) internal glandular and muscular reactions or to (10) overt forms of movements and behavior. Finer divisions in the linkage of the stimulus-response chain may easily be made, but enumeration of the above ten will serve to illustrate the complexity and variety of conditions which must be known before an experience like music can be fully understood.

Before scientific inquiry can pass beyond or below the phenomenal world into the explanatory concepts of physics and physiology, it is essential that the events of the phenomenal world be subjected to some sort of systematic description and classification in order that initial inferences may be made regarding the probable nature of the causes of these events. In many cases these events are presented in sufficiently orderly fashion to make description a simple matter of straightforward observation. Not infrequently, however, classification of phenomenal events is an extremely intricate undertaking, often requiring elaborate experimental technique. Many aspects of musical experience, especially the qualities of sensory material and certain of the simple combinations of these materials, yield readily to description and have long been familiar to physicists, physiologists, and psychologists, as well as musicians. Other aspects which at first glance appear uncomplicated by any difficulties turn out upon further investigation to be extremely puzzling. Is an interval like the fifth always the same at all points of the scale? Musicians would unhesitatingly say yes, whereas observations under laboratory conditions, indicating that such is actually not the case, force psychologists to hold judgment in abeyance.[14]

---

[14] The problem of the phenomenal size of a musical interval was first investigated by C. LORENZ, "Untersuchungen über die Auffassung von Tondistanzen," *Philosophische Studien*, 1891, 6, 26–103. A list of references to the heated controversy between Stumpf and Wundt over this point can be found in TITCHENER, *Experimental Psychology*, 1905, Vol. II, pt. ii, 242. *Cf.* also in this connection C. C. PRATT, "Bisection of Tonal Intervals Smaller than an Octave," *Journal of Experimental Psychology*, 1923, 6, 211–222; "Bisection of Tonal Intervals Larger than an Octave," *ibid.*, 1928, 11, 17–26; and O. ABRAHAM and E. M. VON HORNBOSTEL, "Zur Psychologie der Tondistanz," *Zeitschrift für Psychologie*, 1925, 98, 233–249.

Descriptions of what musical experience is like have come from various sources. To the much abused critic of music, rather than to the musician himself, must go the credit of noting, describing, and clarifying music most effectively. The musician is not only too biased to achieve an attitude of calm contemplation: his very creative and interpretative powers and his incessant preoccupation with matters of technique seem somehow incompatible with the ability to describe musical enjoyment. It was Hegel, I think, who maintained that the musician is the last person in the world to go to for enlightenment about music. Such a statement, even in its exaggerated form, is, of course, no reflection upon the musician. To create or perform a work of art is a greater achievement than to describe one to a philosopher or scientist. "La philosophie est quelque chose; mais la musique, Monsieur, la musique . . . "

The less unruly aspects of musical experience have not only been brought into systematic descriptive order; they have been taken over by the physicist and physiologist as points of departure for the analysis of sounding bodies and of the processes of hearing. Critics, aestheticians, musicians, psychologists, physicists, physiologists, and lovers of music, in general, have all therefore contributed materially to our understanding of tonal art. But as in the case of most psychological exploration, description has far outrun explanation. Auditory sensation, which furnishes the materials of music, is at the present time in a fair way to give up most of its secrets. The data of sensation, however, constitute only a part of music, and beyond the sensory materials lie fertile regions in which all explanation is very tentative indeed, with the result that form and meaning can transcend the descriptive level only at isolated points.

A vast amount of careful work has been done, to be sure, on the description and classification of musical form, so that a systematic treatment of this topic is possible for both psychologists and aestheticians.[15] Psychologists have confined themselves largely to minute analyses of simple auditory integrations, such as are best found in musical intervals. Only from such studies can a beginning be made with the problem of the physiology of sensory form. Critics and aestheticians, on the other hand, proceeding on the assumption that tonal combination was sufficiently well understood for musical purposes, have extended their observations more widely in order to cope with harmony, phrases,

---

[15] C. STUMPF's two-volume work, *Tonpsychologie*, 1883, 1890, presents an elaborate psychological study of tonal combination, fusion, consonance and dissonance, *etc.*, and is generally regarded as a classic in this field.

melodies, counterpoint, and the innumerable variations of large temporal forms exemplified in the
recitative, aria, canzona, gigue, sarabande, alle-
mand, partita, fugue, canon, minuet, scherzo,
rondo, courante, hymn, cavatina, toccata, passa-
caglia, fantasia, waltz, rhapsody, chacono, pas-
torale, bolero, *etc.*, *etc.*[16] No effort will be made in
these pages to multiply the number of words
already expended on this topic. The interested
reader can easily find the literature for himself.

The primary aim of the present section will be to
propound from one or two different angles a character intimately bound up with musical form which,
strangely enough, has been badly neglected, if not
almost completely overlooked, in the many treatises
on musical theory and aesthetics. The nature of
this character can only become clear by illustrations and expositions. Any attempt to formulate
an initial verbal definition would possess little
significance; and the final weight of conviction, if
such there be, can only come, first, by much
listening to music itself, and, secondly, by careful

---

[16] The literature on the technicalities and effects of musical
structure is enormous. E. PROUT's *Musical Form*, 1893, is a
fair example of this literature, much of which displays
exhaustive and careful scholarship. GROVE's *Dictionary of
Music and Musicians* is still the best general source of
reference.

observations under laboratory conditions when crucial examples are well enough known to enable isolation for such purposes. Such observations would be necessary in order to work out the relation between the character in question and the stimulus-conditions (2 in the above stimulus-response chain) which are responsible for its arousal. Enough is already known about form in general to support the assumption that this character, since it is intimately bound up with form, does sustain some sort of functional relation to the stimulus. The uncertainty attaches rather to the quantitative formulation of the relationship. It is therefore legitimate to include it under the general category of form, inasmuch as we have argued that for the sake of clarity only those characteristics which do *not* reveal a relation to the stimulus shall be designated as meanings.

One of the links (9) on the efferent side of the stimulus-response chain will be considered briefly below in connection with the topic of emotion; the last one (10), however, will be left entirely out of consideration. Overt responses to sound-stimuli, or, in other words, the effect of music on behavior, important as the question may be in its own place, are hardly relevant to the present attempt to identify and bring to clearer light certain aspects of music regarded as phenomenal experience. The behavioristic method, stimulating as it has been to general psychology, has up to the present time contributed little of significance to the psychology of music. Does music increase a worker's efficiency? Does it have any therapeutic value? Does the habit of excessive indulgence in music have such a relaxing effect on the character, as James was inclined to believe, that a remedy must be sought by expressing the emotions aroused at a concert through the act of speaking genially to one's aunt (or grandmother, in the *Briefer Course*) or giving up one's seat in a horse car, if nothing more heroic offers? To suggest that this is the only type of question which behaviorism would seek to answer is, of course, unfair. The truth seems rather that behaviorism has not as yet felt inclined to turn to problems in aesthetics.

Errors of commission have been chiefly responsible for the errors of omission with respect to the important characteristic of form which will be considered presently. The natural procedure when facing a new field of investigation is to seek for certain simple uniformities which seem to run through all the complexities and to find out whether the complexities may be regarded as permutations and combinations of the simpler components. Absolutely essential as this method is, there lurks in it a danger. After having hit upon the components which enter into complex objects, the tendency is often to give exclusive attention to these components and to forget entirely the nature of the objects formed by them.

If each possible order in which the letters *A*, *B*, *C*, and *D* may be written is considered a separate object, then there are twenty-four different objects which can be made out of these four letters. Now, if after preliminary exploration of these objects it were soon discovered that in each of them the same four letters appeared (assuming that this was a new field of investigation and that this fact of the four components was not previously known), the danger would be that after this highly interesting and significant discovery had been made all future research would be devoted to an intensive study of the four components with the result that the objects out of which they were extracted would be neglected and their existence practically forgotten. Such an error, I think, has been chiefly responsible for the neglect of certain aspects of musical form. The objects of musical experience are surveyed and it is soon discovered that throughout them all certain typical processes constantly reappear. As a recent text puts it, "When our analysis of music has been completed we shall have found that there are eight factors involved in music: melody, harmony, rhythm, form, tempo, dynamics, tone-color and nuance."[17] True enough, analysis of musical effects will reveal common factors in all of them—possibly more than eight, possibly less. But what about the musical effects themselves? Of what good is it to know all about these factors while remaining forgetful of the effects which led to their discovery?

It will perhaps be well to start with a concrete example. A musical interval is beyond any question of doubt an affair involving, among other things, a difference in pitch of two tones. Therefore pitch-difference is a factor common to all intervals. The laws of pitch-difference in isolation may not, however, be the same as those for pitch-difference in intervals. Reasoning by analogy, then, from one to the other is precarious business, as will be seen from a consideration of some of the arguments advanced by supporters of music making use of intervals smaller than a half-tone.

4. *Division of the Semitone into Smaller Parts*

By combining the notes of the chromatic scale into pairs one has the intervals which form the basis of musical harmony. The smallest interval is the minor second, the two tones of which are a semitone apart, the same distance that separates

[17] J. REDFIELD, *Music*, 1928, 98.

any two adjacent notes of the chromatic scale. In listening to music either in the horizontal direction of melody or in the vertical dimension of harmony there are, therefore, no tonal differences smaller than a semitone, or minor second, which the ear is obliged to take into account. The ear is able, however, to appreciate differences considerably smaller than a semitone. It is undoubtedly this fact which has had much to do with the growing conviction that music fails to utilize all of its available material.

Between the tones of a minor second composed of middle *c* and *c*-sharp there are some thirty-one vibrations; between the tones of the same interval three octaves higher there are two hundred and fifty-one. The tonal combinations which are physically possible within these narrow ranges cannot be explored by the musical system now in use. Hence many people who are not restrained by the belief that any tampering with the present scale is a musical, if not a moral, sacrilege have listened with interest ranging all the way from mild tolerance to extravagant enthusiasm to the efforts and results of experiments with scales and instruments which divide the whole tone into thirds, fourths, eighths, and sixteenths. The most frequent innovation involves the use of quarter-tone intervals. Busoni, however, has experimented with whole tones divided into three parts, and Carrillo has written music and devised instruments for eighths and sixteenths. Perhaps the best-known exponent of quarter-tone music is Alois Hába, the Czech composer.

Many matters of dispute inevitably arise in connection with the radical modification of any system so well and firmly established as the occidental musical scale. It is not infrequently argued that any artist who protests violently against what seem to him the limitations imposed by the sensuous stuff of color, tone, or language, is probably ascribing to his materials the shortcomings which belong to his own inspiration. Botticelli, Palestrina, and Dante managed fairly well the means at their disposal. The artist may reply that the formal sensory structures of an earlier age were entirely adequate to the expression of the aesthetic Idea as it existed in the minds of the great artists of the time, but that with the enormously increased variety and complexity of the items which enter into the psychic life of today there comes the necessity of finding ampler and freer scope in the sensory domain for the effective embodiment of this life in artistic form.

With such questions we shall not here be concerned. The issue before us is simpler, and at the same time more fundamental. It is this: Can the

human ear make adequate discriminations among
tonal intervals which are two, three, or four times
smaller than the minor second? For just as it would
be idle to speculate about the aesthetic effects of
sound-vibrations beyond the range of hearing or of
wave-lengths outside those which correspond to
the perceived spectrum, so would it also be foolish
to waste concern over musical instruments and
compositions which produced subdivisions of a
semitone if it were shown that some of these
subdivisions actually could not be distinguished.

It has already been stated that the ear can
appreciate differences considerably smaller than a
semitone. But to discover the limits of auditory
discrimination is not to settle the question as to
the smallest divisions which may appropriately
be used in constructing tonal intervals. Any two
tones, when sounded simultaneously, form together
an interval, an auditory impression which may or
may not include the awareness of two separate
pitches. Intervals with simple ratios—octaves,
fifths, and fourths—generally approximate a single
unitary impression, whereas the tones of intervals
with more complex ratios, seconds and sevenths,
tend to be less well fused, less unitary. The difference between any two adjacent intervals in the
tempered system of tuning is always the same and
is equal to one-half of a whole tone. A minor sixth,

for example, is a semitone larger than a fifth, a major third, a semitone smaller than a fourth, *etc*. In trying to decide whether it would be practicable to use intervals which lie between the present ones, whether in other words, it would be possible to increase the number of intervals so that any two which were adjacent would be separated from each other by less than a semitone, an important factor is frequently overlooked. It is the neglect of this factor in its numerous ramifications which has introduced confusion not only into discussions of quarter-tone music, but the whole field of music in general.

It might be supposed, since an interval is made up of two tones, that an interval would appear different *qua* interval as soon as a change in pitch of one of the tones was detected. But this is not the case. If it were, it would be correct, other things being equal, to say that the smallest noticeable difference in an interval corresponds to the least perceptible change in one of the components. That which characterizes an interval as such, however, is something more than the mere existence together in consciousness of two tones.

The fifth is made up of the notes *c* and *g*; but the peculiar quality of the fifth which distinguishes it from every other musical interval involves more than the separate auditory qualities of *c* and *g* in combination. "Fifthness," that unique character which every musician recognizes so readily, that musical impression which has something hollow, flat, open, something incomplete and perhaps a bit commonplace about it, can be equated neither to the *c* nor the *g* nor to the mere togetherness of *c* and *g*. No more can the character of the major seventh, with its astringent, gritty, granular, nippy, biting effect, be equated to the sum of the qualities *c* and *b*. None of the differentiating qualities of any of the musical intervals corresponds to the quality of one of the components plus that of the other.

When two tones are sounded together and are recognized as a given musical interval there arises a quality, a relational effect, which must be dealt with in its own right wholly apart from the subsidiary qualities which, under attentive analysis, may be abstracted out of the total experience. To discover the number of intervals between, for example, a fifth and a minor sixth which can be clearly distinguished, it is necessary to determine the least perceptible differences of interval-quality rather than the smallest changes of either of the components. Change in pitch is not correlated point by point with change in interval-quality. Interval-quality may remain the same during an appreciable alteration in pitch. In other words, interval-discrimination and pitch-discrimination are two different things.

The problem of interval-discrimination can be more easily discussed by introducing a unit of measurement which is applicable to all intervals, no matter from what part of the scale they may be taken. The difference between the components of a fifth at the lower end of the scale is 7.9 d.v., while for a fifth at the upper end it is 2,724.5 d.v. To keep these various absolute differences in mind is awkward. The relative differences of the two fifths, however, are exactly the same. The unit for relative tonal difference is called the *cent*. A cent is one-hundredth part of a semitone or one twelve-hundredth part of an octave.[18] All fifths, at any part of the tonal range, are equal to 700 cents, all minor sixths to 800 cents, major thirds to 400 cents, *etc.* The smallest difference in size of interval, either in melodic sequence or in harmonic structure, which the ear is called upon to note is equal to 100 cents. The smallest differences in quarter-tone music would be 50 cents, in eighth-tone music 25, and in sixteenth-tone music 12.5

We come now to the critical point. By a suitable psychophysical procedure it is possible to determine the least perceptible difference in interval-quality, *i.e.*, the range over which an interval may vary without losing its unique and distinguish-

---

[18] *Cf.* HELMHOLTZ, *Sensations of Tone*, 2d ed., 1885, trans. by A. J. Ellis, p. 437, art. 24, xiii, and pp. 446–457.

ing characteristic. The value arrived at in this manner is known as a *limen* or *threshold*, and is defined as that magnitude of physical stimulus which in half the total number of trials will give rise to a perception of difference and in the other half to a perception of no difference. It is a sort of balancing point between sameness and difference. For interval-quality this value is about 20 cents in the middle of the tonal range—that is to say, two intervals are perceived as different when they are separated from each other by no less than 20 cents.[19] It would not be wise to use such intervals in music, however, since, by definition, the people listening to such music would hear modulations in the harmonic structure one-half the time and would be unaware the rest of the time of the subtle changes which the composer had written into his score. Hence it is necessary to calculate from 20 cents, on the basis of the theory of probability, that smallest value of interval which will just be perceived as different 100 per cent of the time. This value comes out just above 50 cents, which

[19] For detailed figures see H. MORAN and C. C. PRATT, "Variability of Judgments on Musical Intervals," *Journal of Experimental Psychology*, 1926, 9, 492–500. Part of the present section is reprinted by permission from my article, "Quarter-tone Music," *Pedagogical Seminary and Journal of Genetic Psychology*, 1928, 35, 286–293.

means that intervals which will uniformly be recognized as different in quality must not be separated from each other by less than a quarter-tone, for 50 cents is equal to a quarter-tone. It would, therefore, be theoretically feasible to double our present chromatic scale so that it would comprise twenty-four quarter-tones instead of twelve semitones; but any further divisions into eighth-tones and sixteenth-tones would be juggling with the mechanics of tuning instruments rather than catering to the psychological capacities of auditory discrimination. The listener to music in which eighths and sixteenths were employed would be generally quite unaware of their presence.

The discriminatory capacity for interval-quality is only one factor, although the most important, which enters into the question of quarter-tone music. It still remains to be known whether, granted that quarter-tone intervals may be distinguished, intervals which lie between the ones now in use would function as independent musical entities, whether they would achieve, during the course of time, the absolute clarity, stability, and recognizable affective values which fourths, fifths, thirds, sixths, seconds, and sevenths enjoy. It is altogether possible that while these intervals might be easily and uniformly recognized as different, they would nevertheless function as musical entities always bearing a relation of subordination or partial assimilation to the nearest fifth, sixth, third, and so on. Such a position might reduce their musical usefulness to the vanishing point. And then picture the confusion of the singer who must make, in some rapid passage, the jump from, say, a major second to the tone a quarter below the major seventh! And still more awful to contemplate: the hysterical anguish of the church organist who must train the soprano who sharps, the alto who porta-ments, the tenor who flats, and the bass who guesses, to sing with tolerable accuracy a quartet in close quarter-tone harmony. And yet such difficul-ties, and the apathy of musical scholars, ought not to stand in the way of those enthusiasts who are convinced that quarter-tone music contains myr-iads of tonal splendors as yet unrealized. Critics and professors have never yet constructed the roads along which the traffic of artistic genius has travelled. These men are only justified in occasion-ally issuing warnings to the artist. In this case they might do well to point out that subdivisions beyond the quarter-tone are out of the question for musical purposes simply because they are indistinguishable to the average listener.

It should be remembered, of course, that there are some individuals who could, most of the time, tell the difference between intervals separated by eighths and even sixteenths, just as there are musicians and people of keen auditory sensitivity for whom equal tempered instruments sound impure and out of tune. For the majority of music lovers, however, subdivisions beyond quarter-tones would have no perceptual existence, although they might produce a vague effect of shifting pitches which, insufficient to establish perception of interval-differences, would nevertheless leave an impression of soft sand-papery sound. Such effects, as a matter of fact, are already secured on pipe organs which have *voix céleste* and *unda maris* stops, by having for each tone two pipes, one of which is out of tune with the other by a beat or two, so that it is really not necessary to resort to an elaborate new system of music to hear the strange ghostly sounds that exponents of sixteenth-tone music seem to cherish. Auditory shimmers, however, are not at all the same thing as stable intervals which can be worked into a system of harmony. To be uniformly perceived as different, two intervals must be separated from each other by at least a quarter-tone. To achieve musical significance and self-sufficiency *may* require separations as large as those now in use.

From such considerations as these it becomes apparent at once that a grave error is introduced when acuity of pitch-discrimination for single tones is taken as a standard for calculating the smallest differences for interval-discrimination. The phenomenal character of a musical interval, although counting among its conditions the stimulus-frequencies of two separate pitches, can not be regarded merely as the summative effect of two simultaneous tones and can not therefore be subsumed under the principles which apply to the perception of single tones. For the latter, pitch-discrimination as low as 8 cents is not at all uncommon in the middle region of the scale, whereas interval-discrimination below 20 cents would be rare indeed. These facts would seem to prove conclusively enough that although differences of pitch are involved in the perception of intervals, these differences are not of the same order as those met with in single tones.

This failure to distinguish sharply between discrimination of single pitches and pitch-discrimination as it enters into the perception of intervals derives from the more general methodological fallacy spoken of in the first part, *viz.*, the identification of the *conditions* of an event with the event itself. Discrimination of pitch is one of the conditions determining the awareness of differences in intervals, but awareness of these differences is by no means identical with pitch-discrimination. More serious consequences of this misinterpretation of the relation of an event to its conditions are to be found in a field of musical investigation which has occupied the attention of a number of psychologists in recent years and has stirred up much controversy and no small amount of opposition among musicians themselves. Although a consideration of this topic will hardly serve to define positively the nature of the characteristic of music which it is the purpose of these sections to elucidate, a clear realization of what this characteristic is *not* will inevitably amount to a partial definition. And since, moreover, the whole problem is speedily becoming of great practical importance to the professional musician, an attempt to make articulate the resentment which many musicians feel towards the psychologist's approach to the problem will certainly not be out of order at this point.

5. *Tests of Musical Talent*

One indication of the validity of any scientific theory may be sought with reasonable assurance in the degree to which the array of facts subsumed under the theory can be successfully put to practical or technological use. Mere knowledge of the existence of a certain fact by no means guarantees the technological value of that fact, for unless the crucial conditions responsible for the occurrence of the fact have been determined it is not possible to know when and how the fact or event will occur again. Description is obviously a first necessary step in all scientific inquiry, but its importance is rapidly superseded by the working out of hypotheses to account for the events described. The test of a hypothesis lies in further description, but description now made more refined and directed by the very terms of the hypothesis itself. If in the light of continued observations the hypothesis seems to hold, then prediction ought to follow as a logical consequence. In spite of the striking changes which are taking place in physical theory today, it is at once obvious, from this point of view, that the older natural sciences possess a very considerable body of indubitable doctrine. If it were not so, technologists could not go ahead safely with their work on bridges, skyscrapers, tunnels, flying machines, talking pictures, *etc.*, *etc.*

In the so-called mental and social sciences the situation is not so favorable. In psychology, at all events, the truth seems to be that the body of well-founded fact, as contrasted with that of dubious opinion, is astonishingly small. In a recent history of psychology

. . . the author confesses to a certain disappointment of his own that experimental psychology has not accomplished more than it has in its seventy years of life. It started with such high hopes that all that was needed was the willingness to experiment, patiently, honestly, and industriously, and it has found that mere faith in experimentalism is insufficient for great and rapid progress, unless that faith is accompanied by some flash of insight as to method. There have been perhaps many little flashes, in addition to the tremendous amount of careful, painstaking research, but there has never been in the history of experimental psychology a dazzling light. Psychology has progressed and developed in a manner similar to the course of any science under ordinary circumstances; but there has not, except for the initial inspiration in the thought of experimentalizing mind, been any great idea or discovery that has revitalized the science—for a science it is—opening up new fields, releasing new energy, and removing hidden doubts.[20]

And yet the pressure upon psychology during the last two decades for quick, practical results has been tremendous, until at the present time purely theoretical studies are not only outnumbered by applied investigations but are pursued with almost an air of apology; with the result that the cart is now generally before the horse, for how can applications reach a desired goal when they lack sound theoretical guidance?

We are repeatedly told that we are living in a psychological age, by which declaration we are presumably to understand that the world has finally accepted the view that if civilization is

[20] E. G. BORING, *A History of Experimental Psychology*, 1929, 659.

worth saving at all mankind must seek for greater control not of that nature which the physical sciences have learned in some measure to subjugate but of that other more unruly nature which reveals itself in human behavior. Statesmen, warriors, politicians, business-men, lawyers, doctors, priests, and teachers are advised to turn to psychology for help, and many psychologists, often even without a tongue in the cheek, go out of their way to tell the world that they are now in possession of a panacea for all human ills.

The mushroom-growth of mental tests is a striking example of the readiness with which psychologists have tried to respond to the demand for practical results. A test for native capacity, a test for acquired practice and information, a test for memory, a test for sound judgment, a test for Boston, another for San Francisco, a positive correlation here, a negative there, all these are found in bewildering array, and the climax of indifference as to what they mean is reached in Pressey's statement that although a large part of his time is spent on tests of intelligence he is not very much interested in the question as to what intelligence really is.[21] Hardly a single

[21] S. L. PRESSEY, "Intelligence and Its Measurement: a Symposium," *Journal of Educational Psychology*, 1921, 12, 144.

activity from the kindergarten to the university has escaped the enthusiastic efforts of some psychologist. Even musical activity has been put to the test.

Although published statements by musicians regarding tests of musical ability are not easy to find, it is my impression, based upon conversations with a large number of musicians, that the musical profession as a whole regards these tests in an unfavorable light. Part of this attitude may unquestionably be ascribed to sheer prejudice: the unwillingness of the artist to have his work interfered with in any way by what he looks upon as the standardization and regimentation introduced by science. Some musicians even entertain the fantastic fear that the meddling activities of psychologists will rob music of its individuality of inspiration. These timid individuals should be assured, of course, that tests of musical talent are not intended, even by their most ardent supporters, to influence in any manner whatever the processes which underlie creative activity. Their sole purpose is to discover, by an examination of the nature of musical experience, whether certain basic characteristics of music are sufficiently susceptible of psychological measurement to be used as reliable indicators of the degree of musical ability which a given individual possesses. It is over this very point, however, that sharp differences of opinion occur. The two quotations which follow may be taken as fairly representing the line of cleavage of these differences: those trained in the atmosphere of the mental tester, tending to accept the results of the tests, and those imbued with the musician's point of view disposed to reject them.

In conclusion I wish to express my own convictions regarding the Seashore Measures of Musical Talent. I feel keenly their unquestionable significance in determining the degree of an individual's musical capacity and have recognized repeatedly the permanency of their prognostic value. As far as their content and technique of construction are concerned they are not excelled. No other test material, to my knowledge, is possible to use year after year in its original form and yet retain its quality of newness and fairness for each person tested. And finally, the basic and fundamental factors measured represent an undercurrent of musicianship *from which all musical expression and interest arise.*[22]

Assuredly, before these tests can be accepted at their face value by the musician, the latter is entitled to an answer to questions like these: Do the standards of measurement arrived at really measure what they claim to measure? Is what they do measure the essence of what enters into

[22] H. M. STANTON, "Seashore Measures of Musical Talent," *Psychological Monographs*, Vol. 39, No. 2, p. 144 (Seashore Commemorative Number: University of Iowa Studies in Psychology, No. 12). Italics mine.

musical aptitude? Are these standards reliable and applicable to all individuals under all circumstances? On the
answers to questions like these, evidently, depends the
practical value of these tests, and with that the place which
the serious-minded musician is justified in assigning to them
within the scheme of his activities . . . Our examination
of the musical capacity tests as at present constituted, then,
has led us to largely negative results. It has demonstrated
the unreliability of some, and the inadequacy of all of these
tests, the greatly exaggerated claims made in their behalf,
their emphasis of the sensorial over the distinctly aesthetic
traits of musical talent . . . To the private teacher . . .
they probably never will discover much that he could not
himself find out very soon in the regular course of instruction, provided he is wide-awake and well-trained.[23]

With the second of these opinions the present
writer finds himself in complete agreement. Not
only are certain of the Seashore tests unreliable
for the purposes for which they were intended; all
of them together fail utterly to get at the kernel of
musical experience. So apparent is this weakness
when once it has been exposed that it would be a
waste of time to labor the point were it not for the
fact that the bold claims of those who sponsor the
tests, together with their priority in the field, have
tended to disarm criticism, especially among those
who will be most seriously affected by them and

[23] J. C. Moos, "The Yardstick Applied to Musical
Talent," *The Musical Quarterly*, Vol. 16, No. 2, 238, 261*f*.

who ought to resist their wholesale application but who, on account of lack of acquaintance with matters pertaining to mental testing, are unable to voice their objection, *viz.*, the musicians themselves.

The uncompromising title of these tests, the fact that the above-mentioned laboratory tests (the motor activities which enter into musical performance) have not been issued in a generally practical form as promised, coupled with the further fact that this test series has been widely used as a complete measure of musical talent without protest on the part of the author, all this has caused this test series to be quite generally accepted as *the* measure, instead of *a* measure, of musical talent.[24]

If the Seashore tests had been designed merely to secure rank orders of individuals with respect to the ability to make the sort of sensory discriminations actually called for in the instructions, no very serious objections could be raised against them, with the exception of the test for consonance.[25] The first test (Pitch) is most certainly a

[24] *Ibid.*, 239.

[25] Those unfamiliar with this work will find a detailed account in C. E. SEASHORE's book, *The Psychology of Musical Talent*, 1919. The phonograph discs upon which the tests are made, together with a manual of instructions, can be secured from the Columbia Graphophone Co. A complete annotated bibliography of the writings of Seashore has been

good clinical measure of pitch-discrimination. The same is true of the second and third tests (Intensity and Time). The fifth test (Memory) may safely be regarded as a reliable index of a person's ability to discover in two series of tones which tone in the second series is different from the one in the corresponding temporal position in the first, and the sixth test (Rhythm) is a satisfactory enough measure of the ability to detect differences in duration and accent in very simple auditory patterns. The fourth test (Consonance), however, is thoroughly unreliable, even for the purpose for which it was designed.

Long before the consonance-test was introduced by Seashore, theoretical and experimental work on auditory fusion had made it clear that judgments upon a tonal interval could be determined by several different potential characteristics of the interval.[26] More recent investigations have brought forth conclusive evidence that only by the most rigid control of instructions can anything like unequivocal

prepared by J. E. BATHURST and R. D. SINCLAIR, *Psychological Monographs*, Vol. 39, No. 2, 3–22 (Seashore Commemorative Number: University of Iowa Studies in Psychology, No. 12).

[26] W. KEMP, "Methodisches und Experimentelles zur Lehre von der Tonverschmelzung," *Archiv für die gesammte Psychologie*, 1913, 29, 139–181.

judgments be secured when bitonal auditory impressions are presented to an observer.[27] If the attitude of the individuals who give the judgments is not carefully controlled by specific instructions, as it certainly can not be when the consonance-test is given to a large number of young people at once, the results have small scientific or even practical significance. And yet this test remains in the Seashore series, in spite of the fact that no person who administers the test can possibly discover from the results what characteristic or trait of the interval has been examined.[28]

The tests in the Seashore series, then, with the exception of that for consonance, are perfectly good clinical measures of the discriminatory capacities indicated by their titles, viz., pitch, intensity, time, tonal memory, and rhythm. Unfortunately,

[27] C. MALMBERG, "The Perception of Consonance and Dissonance," Psychological Monographs, 1918, 25, 93–133; C. C. PRATT, "Some Qualitative Aspects of Bitonal Complexes," American Journal of Psychology, 1921, 32, 490–515. In the second of these studies judgments upon the same tonal intervals were made by the same individuals from at least six different attitudes.

[28] See also, on this point, C. P. HEINLEIN, "An Experimental Study of the Seashore Consonance Test," Journal of Experimental Psychology, 1925, 8, 408–433; and "Critique of the Seashore Consonance Test: A Reply to Dr. Larson," Psychological Review, 1929, 36, 524–542.

however, their purpose is not limited to the measurement of these simple sensory capacities. These tests are supposed to serve as a reliable index of *musical talent* or, in other words, to measure those characteristics present in the experience of a person who is sensitive to musical values. The question really resolves itself into this: is it possible to equate musical experience to the awareness of differences in pitch, intensity, time, consonance, tonal memory, and rhythm?

One adverse criticism which has not infrequently been made against these factors bears repetition. It would be a reasonable assumption, although evidence hardly bears it out, that musical talent or capacity is the unitary functioning of several closely related mental characteristics, such as pitch, rhythm, *etc*. If this were the case, one would expect to find considerable overlap between the members of different pairs of these characteristics, in the sense that a person who secured a high score in one test would also come out with a high score in another, or *vice versa*. This overlap, or presence of common factors among the various traits, would be revealed by high coefficients of correlation. The published results on this point, however, make it appear that high correlations among the tests are the exception rather than the rule. The correlations of various tests with pitch, which Seashore

regards as "the essential medium of musical appreciation and expression,"[29] almost invariably
came to values less than 0.30. For singing the key-
note and for singing various intervals, pitch-discrimination produced values in the region of 0.15!
Can pitch be "the essential medium of musical appreciation and expression" if its influence, as
shown by the tests themselves, is so inconsiderable?
Decidedly not! The fact that a person has a good
ear for pitch no more makes him a musician than
a good eye for color makes him a painter or ability
with figures makes him a mathematician. One can
sympathize with Davison's irritation when he
flares up with the remark that

. . . if William Smith's coefficient of musical expansion is
−28, and the educational doctor tells him that his pitch
sense is deficient, these optimists (those who believe that
most children can learn to appreciate good music) will still
believe that life may yet yield this boy much joy in music
even though he fails to determine the niceties of pitch
variation by a graphophone test that would plunge many a
trained musician into a nervous frenzy.[30]

The best that can be said for the test of pitch
may be epitomized in a threefold interpretation.
Although it is not suited for refined psychophysical

[29] C. E. SEASHORE, *The Psychology of Musical Talent*, 30.
[30] A. T. DAVISON, *Music Education in America*, 1926,
27 *f.*

judgments, the test for pitch-discrimination may be regarded as (1) a good clinical measure of the ability to make discriminations of pitch. No one can take exception to such a statement. To the extent that pitch-discrimination is involved in musical ability, to that extent, *and to that extent alone*, the test may be accepted (2) as a measure of musical talent. The results of the test, when used for this purpose, have already demonstrated, however, that ability to determine niceties of pitch is of small significance in predicting musical talent. Although the correlation of pitch-discrimination with other tests is low, it is nevertheless positive and presumably, therefore, indicates the presence of some factor common to them all. Since the low correlations cause it to be very unlikely that this factor is the overlapping of common group factors of musical ability,[31] it is much more reasonable to suppose that it is related to Spearman's "general factor" of cognition, denoted by the letter g.[32] All of the tests in the Seashore series involve some sort of discrimination. Is it not highly probable, therefore, that *discriminatory* ability rather than *musical* ability produces the positive correlations? From this point of view, however, discrimination is all of a piece with g, and discriminations of pitch,

[31] C. SPEARMAN, *The Abilities of Man*, 340.
[32] *Ibid.*, 74 f.

time, intensity, consonance, changes of tones in sequence, rhythms, *etc.*, are merely specific instances. The test for pitch may therefore be regarded (3) as a measure of discrimination as a function of *g*. Dozens of other tests, however, such as discriminations of lengths of lines, intensities of weights, qualities of odors, *etc.*, would serve the same purpose equally well—and would probably produce correlations with musical ability almost as high as those yielded by the Seashore tests. The same strictures hold for the tests of time, intensity, tonal memory, rhythm, and especially consonance. Their low intercorrelations[33] "must be attributed to *g* alone" rather than to any power which they possess to get at musical talent.

Let the conclusion not be reached too hastily that these adverse criticisms, and the ones to follow, are intended to convey the impression that the Seashore tests possess no value whatever as measures of musical talent. It is obvious, of course,

[33] *Ibid.*, 340. For a more detailed account of these intercorrelations consult C. E. SEASHORE and G. H. MOUNT, "Correlations of Factors in Musical Talent and Training," *Psychological Monographs*, 1918, No. 108, 47–92; R. M. OGDEN, *Hearing*, 309–323; F. M. BRENNEN, "The Relation between Musical Capacity and Performance," *Psychological Monographs*, 1927, 36, 190–262; A. W. BROWN, "The Reliability and Validity of the Seashore Tests of Musical Talent," *Journal of Applied Psychology*, 1928, 12, 468–476.

that pitch, time, *etc.*, are important aspects of music. Any reliable measure of these aspects must therefore yield information which has some bearing on the question of musical talent. But just what is this bearing? The contention has already been made, on the basis of evidence from the tests themselves, that the person with a good ear for pitch (to confine ourselves, for purposes of exposition, to one of the tests) can not be assumed to possess musical talent. He may, or he may not, have musical ability. Then how about the person with a bad ear for pitch? Can one assume with any greater assurance in his case that time spent in the study of music will be wasted than one can assume in the former case that the same amount of time will be profitably spent? When the question is put in this way the answer seems to follow more naturally. A good ear for pitch is no trustworthy evidence of musical ability, but a bad ear for pitch must surely be regarded as a real handicap to musical achievement. The Seashore tests therefore possess what may be called *negative* diagnostic value, in the sense that although they do not speak for those who are endowed with positive musical gifts, they are able to discover those individuals *not* likely to do well in music.

Even this important negative value of the tests must, in actual diagnostic practice, be used with much caution. Since the intercorrelations of the tests and their correlations with the judgments of teachers are so low as to be almost completely equivocal, one concludes that they have not reached the most crucial and significant characteristics of music; in which case one might expect that the results of the tests would depart markedly in two opposing directions from the estimates of musical ability given by teachers. The judgments of the teachers of music regarding the ability of their pupils would presumably be determined to a very appreciable extent by those characteristics which the tests, when administered to these same pupils, fail to discover. Accordingly some of the pupils who ranked high on the tests would be rated lower by the teachers because, in spite of their excellence in the tests, they were thought to lack certain capacities essential to musical success; whereas some of the pupils who ranked not too low would be rated higher because of their possession, in some measure, of these same capacities. In other words, the results of the tests would go to greater extremes in both directions because of their failure to include those characteristics the possession of which would benefit those who did poorly on the tests and the lack of which would injure those who did well. The reverse situation could hardly obtain to any great extent inasmuch as those who did very well or very poorly on the tests could not be graded still better or still worse, respectively, by the teachers.

That this expectation is something more than mere armchair-speculation has been forcefully demonstrated by recent results from the tests themselves.[34] In reporting investigations made with the Seashore tests at the Eastman School of Music, Miss Stanton presents, among other data, the relation between the teachers' estimates of 298 pupils (not 398, unless my arithmetic is at fault) and the scores which these same pupils made on the tests. One half of these pupils tested A or B, the other half, D or E. For those who tested A or B the estimates (in percentages) of the teachers were as follows: A, 14; B, 32; C, 49; D, 1; E, 1; no rating, 3. The teachers' estimates for those who tested D or E were: A, 0; B, 1; C, 45; D, 14; E, 7; no rating, 33. The fact which seemed to make the deepest impression on Miss Stanton was that the teachers tended to rate those who tested D or E lower than those who tested A or B. "Of those who tested D and E, 21 per cent were rated D and E in talent by teachers and only 1 per cent were rated A and B in talent; for those who tested A and B, 46 per cent were rated A and

[34] H. M. STANTON, "Seashore Measures of Musical Talent," *Psychological Monographs*, Vol. 39, No. 2, p. 142.

B in talent and only 2 per cent were rated D and E in talent."[35] Surely one might have expected at least as much agreement as that! Had it been less, the sponsors of the tests would presumably have experienced no little embarrassment. As a matter of fact, however, the agreement is not so impressive as one could wish. One very significant fact about these results apparently escaped Miss Stanton's notice.

What about those students who were rated C by the teachers? Of the A-B group over one half (or 51 per cent) were rated C or lower by the teachers, and 46 per cent of the D-E group were given C or better. The relation between the scores on the tests and the estimates of the teachers appears none too cordial on second glance.[36] The teachers were less than half-way impressed (46 per cent) by those who had met the tests with high success, and unmistakably expressed their conviction that 45 per cent of those who had done badly were just as good as 49 per cent of those

---

[35] *Ibid.*, 142.

[36] Figures which permit of working out a quantitative relation are not given. If one amuses himself, however, with the idle task of applying the Pearson formula $r = \dfrac{\Sigma\, x\, y}{n \sigma_1 \sigma_2}$ to the rank order of percentages, the value turns out to be only about 0.30.

who had done well. And yet, "when these facts were presented to the faculty of the Eastman School of Music in the fall of 1924 a unanimous vote was given that all those who tested D and E should not be admitted to the school, this action to take effect at once."[37] By such methods as these do enthusiastic educational psychologists coerce the honorable profession of teaching into reorganization of curriculum and administration!

How can the discrepancy between the teachers' estimate and the test-results be accounted for? One can not, of course, be certain of the explanation, for the basis upon which the teachers judged is not known, but the presumption is almost irresistible in favor of the view that the teachers formulated their opinions of the students under their charge in terms of those characteristics which lie at the very core of music. As much can not be said of the tests—hence the discrepancy. Pitch, time, intensity, *etc.:* these are all conditions which must be taken into account in an *explanation* of musical effects, but they are not the effects themselves (*cf.* pages 60 f., above). But it is a sensitive appreciation of just these effects that makes the difference between a musically dull and a musically gifted person. Until the tests operate with these effects, the teacher must be regarded as the more

[37] *Ibid.*, 142.

reliable judge of musical talent. He devotes his life to cultivating an appreciation of these effects in his students. His own mind is constantly occupied with them. What is more likely than that he should unfailingly use this accumulated experience as his criterion for estimation of relative excellence among his students? He will have discovered in the first lesson or two whether the student has a good ear, a good sense of rhythm, and some likelihood of telling the difference between a major sixth and a minor seventh; and if his student is adept in these matters the teacher will not immediately jump to the conclusion that a musician has made an appearance. He knows full well that there are more things in music than are dreamt of in the philosophy of music-testers.

The philosophy of intelligence-testing is actually in a healthier state in this respect than that of music-testing, and the latter could profit immensely by taking a leaf out of the books of the former. Whatever adverse criticisms may be leveled against the attempts to measure intelligence, those working in this field are so far, at any rate, free from the accusation of trying to make a simple substitute do the work of the more involved processes of intellectual activity. When it is desired to test reasoning, sound judgment, readiness to detect relationships, memory, analytic powers, *etc.*, the subjects examined are faced with problems and situations the solutions of which actually require the exercise of analysis, memory, ability to discover relationships, sound judgment, and reasoning. When the originators of these tests first began their work it would have been a very natural procedure for them to look about for ways of testing the efficiency of visual and verbal-kinaesthetic processes, for there was at the time an eminently respectable hypothesis to the effect that all higher mental processes are compounds or integrations of simple sensory elements. But they chose to ride roughshod over this hypothesis and make a frontal attack on the higher mental processes themselves rather than on certain sensory elements supposedly abstracted out of them.

Why has it not occurred to those interested in the measurement of musical talent to put music itself to the test? Such an act of simple wisdom, if performed humbly in the interests of theory rather than boldly for the sake of service, might conceivably win some measure of grace from elusive Euterpe.

The impatient desire to be of immediate service is, as a matter of fact, the besetting sin of too many psychologists. The technological value of a fact is ever likely to be dubious until it is fitted into the framework of solid theory. And yet mental testers in general, and those working with tests of

music in particular, rashly make recommenda-
tions for the revision of educational methods on
the basis of scattered facts and figures whose
significance is far from being completely understood. Seashore himself, in treating this very point,
argues that the psychologist who is interested in
practical problems can not afford to let himself
be drawn into a consideration of theoretical
questions![38]

If the demand for help were very urgent indeed,
one might understand and sympathize with such a
disinclination to be drawn into fine points of theory.
In psychopathology, where the need for immediate
action never lets up, it would be fatal for the
practicing psychiatrist to allow moot questions of
theory to retard his decisions. Some attempt to
give practical help is better than no attempt at all.
But where is this urgent need to be found in musical
education? What dire calamity is likely to overtake
the children of the land if for some considerable
time to come the discovery and training of musical
talent are left to the teachers of music themselves?

Training in singing and in the playing of instruments is very largely a matter of private instruction. Without any intention whatever of over-
estimating the excellence of such instruction, one

[38] C. E. SEASHORE, "Measures of Musical Talent,"
Psychological Review, 1930, 37, 178 f.

can reasonably suppose that only the most in-
competent teachers would be unable to do as well
as the tests in estimating whether a pupil was good
enough in his perception of pitch, intensity,
rhythm, *etc.*, to profit by private lessons. And the
better teachers, since they could estimate these
traits in five minutes and would then proceed to
find out whether the pupil had any genuine musical
ability, would do far more than the tests in their
present state can possibly accomplish. Undoubtedly many teachers continue giving lessons to
pupils who fail to profit by them. So do the best
universities in the land. Tests can hardly remedy
this situation any more than they can claim the
discovery of it.

Wherever instruction in music is given along
with other school subjects to large numbers at
once, as in the public schools, the amount of time
devoted to it must of necessity be very small. It is
accordingly improbable that the few pupils for
whom this time is a total loss receive gross undoing
as far as their subsequent careers are concerned.
Since "as a rule children have sufficient musical
ability to profit by ordinary instruction," and since
the tester of musical talent "does not consider it
his mission to discourage,"[39] one is inclined to

[39] C. E. SEASHORE, "Avocational Guidance in Music,"
Journal of Applied Psychology, 1917, 1, 345.

wonder whether the demand for tests of musical talent is really so very great after all. The most that schools can hope to accomplish, and, for the matter of that, the best and finest that they could in all reason ever want to accomplish is to "encourage song as the door through which all may normally enter into active musical enjoyment, and listening as the key to an understanding appreciation of music."[40] No elaborate or technical methods need be put into operation for such a program of instruction. And in the precious little time which can conscientiously be taken from the three R's all pupils should share alike. Further instruction in the intricacies of musical practice and theory lies outside the scope of elementary school instruction and would generally be reserved for those whose musical capacities already take them beyond the reach of the tests. As for the geniuses in music, I dare say even the most enthusiastic tester will grant that such individuals are more likely than not to discover themselves.

The tester of musical talent can therefore afford to return to the cloister of laboratory and study, there to examine more exhaustively the richness of musical experience. If he discovers ways and means of measuring more than the simplest conditions

[40] A. T. Davison, *op. cit.*, 75.

of music, it will then be time to emerge for the purpose of creating a demand for his services.

6. *Types of Aesthetic Judgment*

An investigator into the reasons which people give for liking colors or tones or simple works of art was led to divide his subjects into four types.[41] The persons who liked colors, for example, because they were saturated, pure, or bright, or disliked them because they were thin, mixed, or foggy, he called objective. He judged the color *qua* color. Other individuals liked colors because they called to mind pleasant events, scenes, dresses, objects in nature, *etc.* This type of person he called associative. The physiological, or subjective, type of individual was prone to state his preferences in terms of the effects which the colors made upon him. They soothed him, stimulated him, made him feel excited or uneasy. Still another group of individuals, the *character* type, not always easily distinguished from the objective, reported that they found the colors jovial, calm, cheerful, energetic, *etc.*

The psychological interpretation of these types, with the exception of the last one, offers no par-

[41] E. BULLOUGH, "The 'Perceptive Problem' in the Aesthetic Appreciation of Single Colours," *British Journal of Psychology*, 1908, 2, 406–463.

ticular difficulty. Every object of perception possesses certain intrinsic properties, so that when a person formulates his preferences on the basis of these properties he is being objective in the sense that he confines his judgment to the object regarded as something independent of his own moods and feelings and independent of extraneous associations. When a musician discourses upon the quality of tone production, the forms of harmonic structure, the interlacing of themes in a fugue, and the like, he is objective in this sense. All of these properties are correlated with certain aspects of the stimulus, and are therefore to be included under the materials or form of experience. When, however, an object has come to stand for something else, when a color or picture reminds one of some other event or scene, this phase of the experience can not be related to the aspects of the given stimulus. It is a meaning, as when one is told that a given piece of music represents people entering a church or rustics dancing on the green. Thirdly, any kind of experience may, for some people, set off an emotion. Since an emotion is subjective in the sense that its locus is within the individual rather than external to him, those people who like the emotional bath which certain impressions produce may be called, appropriately enough, subjective.

The classification or interpretation of the character type is not so simple. And yet the judgments given by this type afford, I am convinced, the most significant clew to music's power, give sense and reason to the oft-repeated statement that music is the language of the emotions, and constitute the data which have been all too frequently overlooked by formalists and expressionists alike and neglected entirely by those who seek to measure musical talent. Single tones elicit this type of judgment less readily than do tones in harmonic and melodic patterns. Tonal form, however, is literally saturated with these characters. Even isolated intervals possess them. In addition to the specific arrangement of auditory qualities which enables the musician so easily to identify them as the major seventh, the fifth, or the octave, these intervals are also frequently characterized by the musically sensitive person as being sharp or biting, commonplace or flat, smooth or hollow. More complicated musical structures are referred to as energetic, others as languid, *etc.*

If one takes the trouble to read descriptions of music given by critics, musicians, and lovers of music who attempt to make their experience articulate, he will find, in addition to elaborate technical analysis of the form, abundant use of such words as agitated, calm, wistful, dramatic, seductive, restless, pompous, passionate, sombre, triumphant, and yearning. These characters are more often than not ascribed directly to the music itself. The psychologist, however, likes to guard against the possibility that these are in no true sense objective properties of the music but merely moods and feelings which the listener has erroneously transferred from himself to the music. Upon the settlement of this issue wait many of the disputes in the aesthetics of music. The following sections will attempt to adduce evidence and argument in support of the view that these characters are to be interpreted as objective properties of the musical structure itself.

7. *The Pathetic Fallacy*

Because of the confusion which often surrounds the use of the words "objective" and "subjective" Ruskin, in a moment of irritation, once urged that they be abandoned entirely.

German dullness, and English affectation, have of late much multiplied among us the use of two of the most objectionable words that were ever coined by the troublesomeness of metaphysicians, namely, "Objective" and "Subjective."

No words can be more exquisitely, and in all points, useless; and I merely speak of them that I may, at once and for ever, get them out of my way, and out of my reader's. But to get that done, they must be explained.

The word "Blue," say certain philosophers, means the sensation of colour which the human eye receives in looking at the open sky, or at a bell gentian.

Now, say they farther, as this sensation can only be felt when the eye is turned to the object, and as, therefore, no such sensation is produced by the object when nobody looks at it, therefore the thing, when it is not looked at, is not blue; and thus (say they) there are many qualities of things which depend as much on something else as on themselves. To be sweet, a thing must have a taster; it is only sweet while it is being tasted, and if the tongue had not the capacity of taste, then the sugar would not have the quality of sweetness.

And then they agree that the qualities of things which thus depend upon our perception of them, and upon our human nature as affected by them, shall be called Subjective; and the qualities of things which they always have, irrespective of any other nature, as roundness or squareness, shall be called Objective.[42]

Ruskin then proceeds to demonstrate the manner in which the scope of the subjective is frequently enlarged, "from which position, with a hearty

[42] JOHN RUSKIN, *Modern Painters*, 1856, Vol. III, pt. IV, 157. In order to "meet our German friends in their own style" Ruskin gives, in the first footnote at the bottom of p. 159, a waggish parody of the German philosopher trying to explain the difference between subjective and objective properties of an object. Perusal of it may afford solace to graduate students preparing for examinations in German.

desire for mystification, and much egotism, selfishness, shallowness, and impertinence, a philosopher may easily go so far as to believe, and say, that everything in the world depends upon his seeing or thinking of it, and that nothing, therefore, exists, but what he sees or thinks of."[43] Such lamentable speciousness in no small measure accounts, he thinks, for a bad practice which often creeps into the writings even of the best poets.

Now, therefore, putting these tiresome and absurd words quite out of our way, we may go on at our ease to examine the point in question,—namely, the difference between the ordinary, proper, and true appearances of things to us; and the extraordinary, or false appearances, when we are under the influence of emotion, or contemplative fancy; false appearances, I say, as being entirely unconnected with any real power or character in the object, and only imputed to it by us.

For instance—

"The spendthrift crocus, bursting through the mould
Naked and shivering, with his cup of gold."
                                   Oliver Wendell Holmes.

This is very beautiful, and yet very untrue. The crocus is not a spendthrift, but a hardy plant; its yellow is not gold, but saffron.

Thus, for instance, in Alton Locke,—

"They rowed her in across the rolling foam—
The cruel, crawling foam."

[43] *Ibid.*, 158.

The foam is not cruel, neither does it crawl. The state of mind which attributes to it these characters of a living creature is one in which the reason is unhinged by grief. All violent feelings have the same effect. They produce in us a falseness in all our impressions of external things, which I would generally characterize as the "Pathetic fallacy."[44]

This practice of ascribing to things characters which they do not actually possess is a familiar enough one. It is commonly recognized as poetic license, and its scope in this field of writing is undoubtedly much wider than Ruskin would approve. Even when Monsieur Jourdain talks it occasionally makes an appearance. In a great many instances of its use there can be no doubt whatever that, regarded from the point of view of strict truth, it represents a fallacy.

Suppose, for example, that in spite of my most painstaking efforts to execute a powerful stroke, the golf ball rolls ingloriously from the tee. I then turn and rend my new driver or call down maledictions upon it. I am angry not with myself but with it. I feel resentment toward it precisely as though it had meant to spite me. I virtually attribute malice to it. Now this, as my less heated partner may remind me, is unreasonable, because the golf-stick really did not mean it, or do it on purpose.[45]

In such a case the anger plainly belonged not to the stick but to the person who wielded it inglo-

[44] *Ibid.*, 159 *f.*
[45] R. B. PERRY, *General Theory of Value*, 1926, 56.

riously, and the malice was erroneously transferred from the latter to the former. By no means does it follow, however, that whenever a situation is described in terms of so-called human characters "the reason is unhinged by grief" or "under the influence of emotion, or contemplative fancy." The practice against which Ruskin inveighs is not always pathetic. Neither is it a fallacy.

8. *Subjective vs. Objective*

Out of the totality of my experience while I am writing these lines it is a simple matter to abstract certain aspects, primarily visual in nature, which with all appropriateness may be called objective. These aspects range in clearness from the black letters and words left by the type-bars as they strike the paper on the roller of the typewriter, through the keys of the board and my fingers moving over them, to paper, books, pencils, matches, and other objects lying about on the table. All of these impressions are given directly in visual perception and are objective in the sense that they are immediately localized as "out there" in space. Certain other impressions, however, reach me with an internal local sign upon them. They are within the body and for that reason may appropriately be called subjective.

Chief among these impressions is a sense of uneasiness which I ascribe to the conflict between my desire to finish this section and the necessity of leaving it abruptly if I am to keep an unwelcome appointment. I am certain enough of the uneasiness, and I am equally certain, when I give attention to it, that its locus is inside this object which I call my body, not outside of it. In fact, I can describe and localize it roughly as a sort of dull dragging pressure which begins somewhere in the lower region of the chest and settles down heavily into the pit of the stomach.

So suitable do the words "subjective" and "objective" seem for the marking off of these two types of experience that at the risk of offending those who might agree with Ruskin as to their exquisite uselessness and in spite of the confusion which they create in other contexts, they will be retained in these sections for the purpose of signifying a difference which will presently assume considerable importance in treating of the relation of the pathetic fallacy to music. No other difference is intended in the use of these words than that described in the preceding paragraph. Nothing whatsoever about the ultimate nature of these two types of experience is at all implied. Certain events within the totality of experience appear external to the body. Other events are localized within the body. The former are objective, the latter subjective. That is all. This particular distinction, moreover, is one which has recently been emphasized by Köhler who assures his readers that long before he was aware of elaborate philosophical distinctions

. . . there were innumerable varieties of experience appearing as "objective," *i.e.*, as existing or occurring independently and externally. There were other experiences which belonged to me personally and privately, and insofar were "subjective," such as, among others, dreadful fear upon certain occasions, and an overwhelming, warm happiness at Christmas.[46]

Dreadful fear, overwhelming happiness, worry, anxiety, uneasiness—these variations in emotional states fall unequivocally in the category of the subjective. And yet, according to some of Bullough's observers and also to Ruskin's doctrine of the pathetic fallacy, these subjective characters, these moods and feelings, are not infrequently spoken of as though they were actual properties of objective states. On the assumption that there can be no real confusion of emotions and objective states, is such easy transposition merely *in dictione*, or, what would be far more critical for aesthetic theory, can the transposition, as the result of

[46] W. Köhler, *Gestalt Psychology*, 1929, 20 *f*.

properties common both to subjective and to objective experience, be truly *extra dictionem?* The question becomes even more timely in the light of recent experimental studies of emotional behavior in which, of all places, the distinction between objective and subjective is completely lost sight of, with what beclouding of theoretical issues will be seen in a moment.

At the very beginning of Part I it was said that aesthetic experience could be conveniently divided into three parts, material, form, and meaning. A fourth division, for emotion, should, of course, be made whenever this important subjective phase of the enjoyment of art receives consideration. In the present volume, however, emotions, as such, will be left out of account. The reason for this seemingly cavalier treatment of so important a topic is simple and legitimate enough. Not the effect upon the passions and moods and sentiments, but the nature of music itself is here the problem. That the former may be excited in varying degrees of intensity by music is not denied, but that an analysis of these will reveal the nature of music is doubtful. Music may very well be the food of love, it may have charms to soothe the savage breast, and the man not moved by it may be fit for treasons, stratagems, and spoils, and be possessed of affections dark as Erebus; but these facts, if such they be, have little or no bearing upon the proper nature of music itself, except in so far as one may wish to enumerate them as among the things which music can *do*—as contrasted with what music *is*. Music will also make some people tap their feet, but that fact bears about the same relation to music as the hole in the ground made by the falling stick of a skyrocket does to the gorgeous display which preceded it. And yet so badly mixed up in the minds of some people have these two relatively independent aspects of music become, that all too frequently the sole and great aim of music is said to be the arousal of the emotions—according to which standard the sphere-descended maid assumes a position very considerably inferior to a game of poker.[47] The arousal of emotions by music is, naturally enough, a very real psychological problem, but it is not the problem with which this book is primarily concerned.

In spite of the irrelevance of actual emotional states to the question as to what music itself is

[47] A searching inquiry regarding the rôle of emotion in music has been made by EDUARD HANSLICK in his famous little book, *The Beautiful in Music* (trans. 1891 by G. Cohen from seventh German editon). At the end of the first chapter Hanslick cites quotations from some twenty authors who have confused music with its emotional effects.

like, the topic can not be dismissed in a mere paragraph. Whenever emotions are mentioned in connection with music, two very different issues are likely to become confused. If it is maintained that music stirs the emotions, sets into action certain subjective experiences different from the music heard, that is one issue, but an issue which can be put aside in the present study. When, on the other hand, it is said that emotions are the *subject-matter* of music, an entirely different issue is raised. The implication here seems to be that in music, as heard, the emotions are somehow embodied or portrayed; as though sounds, which are surely fully as objective as sights, could become the medium for the delineation of organic and kinaesthetic processes, for to such as these must the subjective (meaning by that, bodily sensations) be capable of reduction. Is this a pathetic fallacy? Are we here confronted with the reading into music of a character which, strictly speaking, has been erroneously transferred from the subjective to the objective?

9. *Emotion*

If emotion is truly the sort of subjective experience that it is here represented to be, it should follow that an analysis of it would reveal the presence of bodily processes, for in the present context subjective experience is to be regarded as coextensive with those psychological events which have their locus within the body. As a matter of fact, this very contention, namely, that the emotion, as felt, must be within the body, forms the central theme of a famous theory in psychology. In 1884, and again in 1890, William James (and at about the same time, C. Lange, the Danish physiologist) elaborated his argument that the bodily changes, which psychology had long recognized as in some way intimately bound up with emotional life, instead of being caused by the emotion, *"follow directly the perception of the exciting fact, and that our feeling of the same changes as they occur IS the emotion."*[48]

Numerous passages make it clear beyond all doubt that if the subjective is equated to bodily process, then the James-Lange theory is assuredly dealing with a subjective affair. "The various permutations and combinations of which these organic activities are susceptible make it abstractly possible that no shade of emotion, however slight, should be without a bodily reverberation."[49] "Our whole cubic capacity is sensibly alive; and

[48] W. JAMES, *The Principles of Psychology*, 1890, Vol. II, 449.

[49] *Ibid.*, 450.

each morsel of it contributes its pulsations of feeling, dim or sharp, pleasant, painful, or dubious, to that sense of personality that every one of us unfailingly carries with him."[50] "A purely disembodied human emotion is a nonentity . . . The more closely I scrutinize my states, the more persuaded I become that whatever moods, affections, and passions I have are in very truth constituted by, and made up of, those bodily changes which we ordinarily call their expression or consequence."[51]

In spite of numerous objections which have been urged against the James-Lange theory, it is probably safe to say that most psychologists would still attach great weight to the views therein expressed. At all events, the importance of bodily states in emotion (and therefore its subjective character) is recognized without question.[52] That these bodily states *are* the emotion is less plausible than that

[50] *Ibid.*, 451.

[51] *Ibid.*, 452.

[52] The authors of the most recent text-book I have seen state near the beginning of the chapter on feeling, emotion, and volition, "We now come to a different kind of experience—experiences which result chiefly from *systemic* stimulation. These experiences are concerned, first and foremost, with the *condition of our bodily organism*—not with events in the surrounding world." H. C. WARREN and L. CARMICHAEL, *Elements of Human Psychology*, 1930, 227.

they are among the *conditions* of emotion. Emotions presumably exist for the majority of people without an immediate awareness of bodily disturbance. Hence emotions and bodily states are not identical or perfectly interchangeable. Only the insistence with which the latter turn up when emotion is subjected to more careful scrutiny leads to the conclusion that they are chiefly responsible in determining the nature of emotional experience.

This slight modification of the strict letter of James's interpretation does not, however, alter the subjectivity which characterizes felt emotion. A very radical modification, or rather, an almost complete misunderstanding of the James-Lange position, however, is introduced when objections are raised to the theory on the basis of observations made upon emotional *behavior;* when, in other words, the term "emotion" is used indiscriminately to cover two very different sorts of phenomena. It is perfectly legitimate, of course, to use the word in both senses provided some indication is given regarding the difference, as when one says, "*Emotion* is a name given (1) to certain bodily states observable in another and (2) to certain experiences known by introspection."[53] James unquestionably used the word in the second of these meanings. Studies made upon the phenomena included in

[53] *Ibid.*, 232.

the first of these meanings do not, therefore, necessarily bear at all upon the kind of emotion with which James was concerned. And yet the results of recent studies in emotional behavior have been freely cited as evidence against the validity of the James-Lange theory. Since an attempt must be made to mark off the type of emotion comprehended in this theory from the character of objective musical structure, it will be well to risk a digression at this point in order to demonstrate, if possible, the irrelevance of the strictures brought against the theory by those interested in emotional behavior.

Cannon, whose famous studies of emotional behavior in animals are well known to psychologists and physiologists, raises five specific objections to the James-Lange theory.[54] These objections will be considered separately, and in the order given by Cannon.

---

[54] In this very brief critique of Cannon it will be assumed that the reader is familiar with the main lines of evidence which Cannon uses. Those interested in the subject, but unacquainted with the literature, should consult W. B. CANNON, *Bodily Changes in Pain, Hunger, Fear and Rage*, 1915 (revised edition, 1929), and his article "The James-Lange Theory of Emotions: A Critical Examination and an Alternative Theory," *American Journal of Psychology*, 1927, 39, 106–124.

a. Total separation of the viscera from the central nervous system does not alter emotional behavior.[55] Cannon's sympathectomized cats and Sherrington's dogs whose lungs, heart, stomach, bowels, spleen, liver, and other abdominal organs were disconnected from the brain all behaved with full emotional expression in the presence of appropriate stimuli. From this very important fact one may draw the conclusion that these particular responses (called "emotional expression") do not depend upon the proper functioning of the viscera, and that they are probably for the most part unlearned responses adequately accounted for in terms of reflex theory. It is entirely conceivable that they could be set off in the complete absence of what would be called emotional experience in man. Cannon admits that "we have no real basis for either affirming or denying the presence of 'felt emotion' in these reduced animals," but in the very same paragraph in which this statement is made he says that "operations which, in terms of the theory, largely or completely *destroy emotional feeling,* nevertheless leave the animals behaving as angrily, as joyfully, as fearfully as ever."[56] The very point at issue is whether this emotional

[55] W. B. CANNON, "The James-Lange Theory of Emotions," *American Journal of Psychology*, 1927, 39, 108.

[56] *Ibid.*, 109. Italics mine.

feeling is destroyed! From the results of the experiments one can only conclude that a certain type of behavior has not been destroyed or altered. The evidence has no bearing on emotional feeling.

b. The same visceral changes occur in very different emotional states and in non-emotional states.[57] In view of this fact the suggestion has often been made that marked differences between emotions may be due to the conformation, supplementary to the visceral changes, of the proprioceptive patterns. Even if this suggestion should fail, there is still another possibility which must be disposed of before this particular fact of diffuse visceral action can count against the James-Lange theory. Although the same visceral changes occur in very different emotional states, no evidence has yet been given that they all occur with the same relative intensity in each different emotion. If they do not, this fact might well be at the basis of emotional differences. A parallel situation is found in the stimulus-conditions which determine differences in auditory timbre. Two different instruments may possess the same partials, but these partials may be present with different relative degrees of intensity. The oboe and the split tone of the French horn, for example, both have the same partials,

[57] *Ibid.*, 109

namely, the first twelve. But in the case of the oboe 66 per cent of the total intensity is concentrated in the fourth and fifth partials, whereas in the case of the horn the total intensity is distributed much more uniformly over all twelve partials. Now if difference in relative intensity of the same partials can make all the difference between the tone of an oboe and the split tone of a French horn, surely differences in the relative intensity of preganglionic stimulation leading to change in action of arterioles, blood sugar, digestive glands, heart, adrenin, gastro-intestinal peristalsis, *etc.*, might readily account for the differences between, let us say, joy and anger. Certain non-emotional states also "are known to induce *most* of the changes"[58] found in emotional states. If *all* of the changes, in their proper relative intensities, were induced, would the experience then be non-emotional?

c. *The viscera are relatively insensitive structures.*[59] Even if it were demonstrated that the viscera are completely insensitive, the fact of felt bodily disturbance in the face of an emotional situation would not thereby be altered in the slightest. James rested his case chiefly on the abundant evidence supporting this fact. His theory is therefore untouched by this third objection.

[58] *Ibid.*, 110. Italics mine.
[59] *Ibid.*, 111.

d. Visceral changes are too slow to be a source of emotional feeling.[60] The evidence on this point must surely be regarded as inconclusive. Cannon cites the following times for the latent period of smooth muscle, as given by different investigators: 0.25 second, 0.8 second, 0.85 second, 2 to 4 seconds, 3 seconds, and 6 minutes. The only figures which he gives for emotional reaction-times are taken from affective judgments upon pictures of men and women and upon odors. These times were around 0.8 second. It is more than likely that these judgments were based on feeling, not emotion—a distinction which Cannon appears to have overlooked. Even if they were judgments of emotion, their time of 0.8 second is not shorter than some of the times for the latent period of smooth muscle.

e. Artificial induction of the visceral changes typical of strong emotions does not produce them.[61] Even if one were to hold to the strict letter of James's statement that our feeling of the bodily changes as they occur *is* the emotion, the fact that artificial induction of visceral changes does not produce emotion would not tell against James, for numerous bodily processes in addition to those

[60] *Ibid.*, 112.
[61] *Ibid.*, 113.

from the viscera make their appearance in emotional excitement. Since injection of adrenin does not bring these into play, it could not be expected to give rise to a full-blown emotion. The remarkable feature about experiments like those of Marañon is not that injection of adrenin failed to create a real emotion but rather that the subjects in the experiment came as close as they actually did to having a real one. They reported feeling as if awaiting a great joy, as if afraid, as if they were going to weep without knowing why, as if something were about to happen to them, as if possessed of a great fright, *etc*. Such statements as these sound as though the experiment in artificial synthesis, even with many of the elements left out, had almost succeeded. Instead of ruling the viscera out, the experiment tends to confer upon them the status of essential, though not the sufficient, conditions of emotion.

Cannon's own theory of emotion need not detain us, chiefly for the reason that one can not tell which of the two kinds of phenomena included under the single term "emotion" his theory is intended to explain. His experimental work has been directed towards the study of emotional *behavior*, whereas his theorizing is very much concerned with emotion as felt experience. It is difficult to understand how the latter can be comprehended within his theory, for by burning his kinaesthetic and organic bridges behind him Cannon has nothing left to account for the subjectivity of felt emotion. "*The peculiar quality of the emotion is added to simple sensation when the thalamic processes are roused.*" Where, one may ask, is this "peculiar quality of the emotion," this contribution of "glow and color to otherwise simply cognitive states," this "aura of feeling" added to sensations?[62] Surely not in the thalamus, for one can not feel his own thalamus. If, on the other hand, they are part and parcel of bodily sensation, they fall outside the scope of Cannon's theory and lend further support to the position upheld by James. One is led to conclude, therefore, that the James-Lange theory "is so strongly fortified by proof and so repeatedly confirmed by experience that it cannot be denied substantial truth. In spite of elaborate refutations it shows no signs of obsolescence."[63]

[62] *Ibid.*, 120 *f.*

[63] R. B. PERRY, *op. cit.*, 295. Since the above comments on Cannon's objections to the James-Lange theory were written, a much more thorough criticism of Cannon's position has appeared—E. B. NEWMAN, F. T. PERKINS, and R. H. WHEELER, "Cannon's Theory of Emotion: a Critique," *Psychological Review*, 1930, 37, 305–326.

10. *Aesthetic Emotion*

Having found no good reason for doubting the subjectivity of felt emotion, we may now consider for a moment a view of emotion which is peculiar to aesthetics. In the history of aesthetic theory the topic of emotion has either been neglected entirely (one may search numerous works of aesthetics without finding a single reference to emotion) or has been treated in a manner markedly different from that usually accorded the subject in general psychology. The reason for slighting the topic is presumably similar to that given for passing over emotional effects of music in the present volume. Works of art may, for many people, give rise to emotional experiences of one sort or another, but the analysis of a work of art, as such, is not advanced by an examination of the emotional effects which it produces in the person who beholds it. When, on the other hand, the attention of aestheticians has been directed to the emotional effects of art, the conclusion has generally been drawn that these effects are somehow different from *real* emotions; that, in other words, there is such a thing as a distinctly *aesthetic* emotion.

In the very earliest speculations about art this distinction between real emotions and the emotions of art was vaguely sensed. Much labor and learning have been devoted to the discovery of what Aristotle meant by κάθαρσις. This much seems certain. In common with other Greek writers on aesthetics, Aristotle was unable to rid himself of the view that art is an imitation of reality and, as such, is subject to the same laws, and responsible for the same human attitudes as any real event in actual life. But his reference to the alleviating discharge or purification of fear through pity and his insistence upon the transfiguration and idealization of tragic emotion into noble pleasure have led to the view that he must have related "aesthetic emotion to the self widened into humanity."[64] The emotion is softened—made more a matter of intellect than of feeling—so that the spectator of tragedy *comprehends* the emotional circumstance but is not himself infected by it.

German aestheticians, especially Hartmann, often speak of *Scheingefühle*, emotions which, although having their origin in lively and vivid perceptions, are, because of the detachment of aesthetic contemplation, unreal and illusory as compared with the emotions of everyday existence. Recent English writers, following Bullough, not infrequently express similar views in terms of psychical distance. All things which concern human action range between two extremes of emotional

[64] B. BOSANQUET, *A History of Aesthetic*, 1904, 428.

appeal. Many events find the human organism
prepared for strong emotional response. They strike
what the Freudians would call a complex. For
obvious reasons the king in *Hamlet*, when he
watches the dumb-show of the players, is too
violently upset to sit through the speeches which
follow. At the opposite extreme lie those happenings
which offer dead options to human choice. The fate
of peoples in distant lands, for example, is generally
too remote to call forth natural understanding and
sympathy. True aesthetic appreciation, so the
argument runs, is best found midway between
these extremes. An object, when contemplated as
a work of art, should not stir up the emotions. All
sorts of events outside of art accomplish this end
more successfully, but at the same time the eye for
any loveliness of material and form which may
exist within these events becomes clouded by the
underdistance of emotional preoccupation with
their practical consequences. Neither should an
event be so overdistanced that it loses contact with
all human values. The emotions in art, then, are
neither real nor unreal. Aesthetic emotions belong
in a class by themselves.

James includes aesthetic feelings under what he
calls the subtler emotions. It is a pity he did not
feel inclined to elaborate this theme at greater
length, for in the sentence or two in which he states

(and then dismisses the subject) that certain so-called aesthetic feelings are not emotions at all he has drawn a distinction long urgently needed, but almost completely overlooked in the psychology of art. Whenever it is a question of these subtler emotions,

> . . . unless there be coupled a bodily reverberation of some kind with the mere thought of the object and cognition of its quality; unless we actually laugh at the neatness of the demonstration or witticism; unless we thrill at the case of justice, or tingle at the act of magnanimity; our state of mind can hardly be called emotional at all. It is in fact a mere intellectual perception of how certain things are to be called—neat, right, witty, generous, and the like. Such a judicial state of mind as this is to be classed among the awarenesses of truth; it is a *cognitive* act. As a matter of fact, however, the moral and intellectual cognitions hardly ever do exist thus unaccompanied. The bodily sounding-board is at work, as careful introspection will show, far more than we usually suppose. Still, where long familiarity with a certain class of effects, even aesthetic ones, has blunted mere emotional excitability as much as it has sharpened taste and judgment, we do get the intellectual emotion, if such it can be called, pure and undefiled.[65]

The absence of a reverberating bodily sounding-board in the experience of a trained artist is indicated, says James, in Chopin's superlative of praise of new music, "*Rien ne me choque.*"

[65] W. James, *op. cit.*, 470 *f.*

While one may not be inclined to agree with James that the experience of the expert in art tends to be dry and pale in comparison with the sentimental layman, it is an idea worth entertaining that much of his experience that goes by the name of emotion is, strictly speaking, not emotion at all, but a property of objective experience, a character which resides within the object as perceived. Such a line of division by no means robs aesthetic contemplation of all glow and warmth.

Psychologists have long felt justified in making a distinction between feeling and emotion, although the terms are frequently used interchangeably. Feeling is a single dimension of experience ranging between two maximal opposites, pleasantness and unpleasantness, through a point of indifference. Emotions are qualitatively distinguishable from one another; feelings align themselves on a single intensive continuum, yielding judgments simply of "more" or "less." It would seem to be axiomatic that when a person *enjoys* a work of art he experiences pleasantness, and that the more he enjoys himself the greater the pleasantness. Intense enjoyment and pleasure are frequently referred to, in popular speech, as rapture, elation, delight, transport, exultation, ecstasy, *etc.*, whereas in psychology these names would more generally be regarded as variations on the single theme of intensive pleasantness. Be that as it may, it surely will be granted that intense pleasure may exist in the absence of what James would call the coarser emotions, and that if such pleasure exists, experience is not destitute of all glow and warmth.

Now although James was quick to sense the difference between the emotions which he sought to explain by his famous theory and the kind of experience one frequently has in the presence of a work of art, he made confusion worse confounded by calling the latter an *intellectual emotion*. It would have been far better if he had held to the statement that often in the presence of a work of art "our state of mind can hardly be called emotional at all." If it is extremely doubtful that one's state of mind can legitimately be called emotional at all, matters are not helped by suggesting that this non-emotional state is an intellectual emotion. Would it not be better to examine critically the hypothesis that many experiences bearing a superficial resemblance to emotion, particularly those which have gone by the name of aesthetic emotions, are simply not emotions at all and should therefore not be dealt with under the heading of emotion? If this were to turn out to be the case, the question would immediately arise as to how non-emotional states can possibly resemble emotions. How can objective experiences (non-emotional states) be so easily confused with certain subjective experiences (emotional states) that the practice of describing the former by words which also apply to the latter is condemned as a pathetic fallacy?

11. *Similarities between Objective and Subjective Experience*

If one were to seek an understanding of the confusion which exists between such apparently disparate fields as objective (visual and auditory) and subjective (organic and kinaesthetic) experience it would be quite natural to ask whether these fields both possess characteristics sufficiently alike to account for the confusion. Marked similarities undoubtedly do exist, but the almost unavoidable practice of psychologists of working out their problems within the more or less rigid limits set by the necessities of classification tends to obscure the similarities and accentuate the differences. Vision, audition, taste, smell, and the bodily sensations all have their own special problems and methods, and the more intensively they are pursued the more they become segregated into their own compartments. In addition, therefore, to the very obvious differences which exist among the sense departments one must reckon also with the somewhat artificial lines of demarcation created by the exigencies of scientific study.

From one angle of regard the qualities of any pair of sense departments are as far apart as the east is from the west. It would certainly be cause for wonderment if an individual were to mistake smells for pressures, sounds for visceral sensations, or colors for tastes. All senses, however, have certain attributes in common, and if these attributes function in the same way for two different sensations, some degree of similarity is thereby created. A sound which increases steadily in intensity during an interval of five seconds has something in common with a pressure which becomes uniformly more intense during a like interval of time. Other characteristics, less generally recognized as simple attributes, also attach to several different sense departments. Bright, dull, sharp, and big are words which apply both to sounds and to pressure. And Köhler quotes with approval the German poet Morgenstern who states that *"Die Möwen sehen alle aus, als ob sie Emma hiessen."*[66]

Not, however, by comparing the qualities of simple sensory material itself does one encounter the most striking examples of cross-modality likenesses. It is in the *form* of different sensory materials that similarities make their appearance most frequently. In the visual field a circle, for example, may be

[66] W. Köhler, *Gestalt Psychology*, 1929, 242.

red, blue, green, yellow, or any other color, and yet in each case the form is identified as the same. But the circle may also appear in an entirely different sense department, for tactual material presents spatial contours which, as far as the form is concerned, are recognized as identical with those in vision. Even more pronounced are the similarities of form in rhythms from different sense modalities. Exactly the same rhythms, together with any variations in accent and tempo, may be set up in audition, vision, and touch, and whatever of sturdiness, lightness, heaviness, steadiness, or what not, characterizes the rhythms from one sense must also appear in the others. Even these few examples, among innumerable others which might be cited, make it clear that the different sense departments are not separated by impassable barriers. Nor, it should be added, does it serve the interests of scientific parsimony to argue that in these cases the easy passage from one modality to another is accomplished by the indirect routes of association or analogy.

Association by similarity and inference by analogy are principles which have long held an honorable place in the literature of psychology. In using them one must be careful, however, to recognize just what they mean. When two events are associated on the basis of similarity, as when one says that the consequences of the World War remind him of the great fight told to little Peterkin, either of those events, because of certain points in common with the other, is likely, when thought of, to bring the other one to mind. The similarity which exists between the two events is itself, however, not the product of association, but only the datum which, under certain conditions, gives rise to association. The similarity is a matter of direct observation. It may, however, never be observed, or, if observed, it may never lead to association, and yet the properties which are potentially capable of being viewed within the relation of similarity exist in their own right whether they are seen in this particular relation or not. Thus in the extreme case of the circles in two sense departments in which similarity amounts to practical identity, it is obvious at once that the perceiving of tactual circularity is not the product of association with visual circularity. Circularity is common to both modalities and may be directly perceived in either one without the intervention of any association whatsoever with the other. By the same token, a given musical phrase may remind one of a graceful dancer, but before assuming that when one says that the musical phrase itself is graceful he has erroneously read into the phrase certain characters which belong only to the movements of the dancer, the fact must be faced that the one would not have called up the other unless each had possessed certain characters in common. Gracefulness is a property which belongs somewhere in direct experience, and there is no *a priori* reason to suppose that visual form holds exclusive rights to it.

Yet one may argue still further, as a last resort, that gracefulness, strictly speaking, is a property neither of visual nor of auditory form, but is a character which is erroneously transferred to these fields from certain qualities which one feels in the movements of his own body. Here, indeed, would be the pathetic fallacy, the ascription of characters to visual and auditory processes which belong strictly only to bodily sensations.

Even when the body is not actually moving about, the sensations which come from it are frequently shot through with movement. One may be startled while sitting perfectly still, but at the same time he will probably feel a rush of hot pressure all over, a sinking in the pit of the stomach, a rapid beating of the heart, and shivers and trembling down his spine and legs. When the body is in movement, awareness of this movement in kinaesthetic terms follows as a matter of course. This prevalence of movement in the kinaesthetic and organic fields is undoubtedly chiefly responsible for the large number of words which, when used to describe how one feels, signify the variations in the dynamic, active character of movement. Forceful, weak, languid, agitated, restless, calm, excited, quiet, indecisive, graceful, awkward, clumsy, tripping, rhythmic, fluent, and so on through a long list, are all words which appropriately characterize how one feels when he encounters various situations. Since, however, these words fit the qualities of felt bodily movement, it would not be a pathetic fallacy to use them for movements in other sensory fields, unless these latter movements were devoid of the characters found in bodily movement, which hardly seems likely.

A swift, uneven, agitated, upward movement, increasing rapidly in intensity, may run through visual sensation, auditory sensation, and bodily sensation, giving to all three a similar form, and the perception of this form in any one of these fields does not depend upon inference by analogy nor association by similarity, inasmuch as the same form exists in all three alike. Thus gracefulness may be given intrinsically either in visual or in auditory movement, quite apart from the fact that it may also be perceived as a property of felt bodily movement. One may understand, then, the confusion which often arises between objective and subjective experience, for the similarities between them are frequently very marked, so much so that a great many words apply to both equally well and, contrary to the doctrine of the pathetic fallacy, equally accurately.

12. *Movement in Music*

When one tone is followed by another tone of different pitch, the second tone is not only heard as higher or lower in pitch than the first, it is also perceived as the end of an upward or downward movement. If the number of tones is increased, the movement is correspondingly prolonged, and the only limitations to complexity of moving tonal forms are those set by the range of pitch of the human voice or of orchestral instruments, the speed with which the tones may be executed, the width of interval between tones, the possible variations in rhythm, ascent, and tempo, and the number of separate moving parts which may be used simultaneously with any degree of effectiveness. The musician will at once recognize how almost limitless the variety of movements in music can be. Descriptions of music reflect this variety in the use of such words as: rise, fall, ascend, mount, leap, bound, spring, shoot, tower, soar,[67] surge, drop,

[67] *Aufschwung* is the title of one of Schumann's piano compositions, *Op.* 12, No. 2.

sink, slide, swoop, tumble, shift, swerve, tremble, quiver, flutter, pulsate, *etc*. And the use of the word "movement" for differences in tempo and rhythm, as well as the divisions of the sonata and symphony, need hardly be regarded as a derived meaning.

Yet something in the nature of auditory move-ment seems to set it apart from other kinds of movement. Occasionally one may even hear doubt expressed whether it is legitimate to speak at all of movement in music. The weight of majority opinion, however, runs overwhelmingly counter to such doubt. A difference nevertheless does exist, and although careful inquiries into the nature of this difference have not been made, casual obser-vation can point to certain factors which must have something to do in giving to auditory move-ment its individual character.

Visual movement consists in the rapid shifts in spatial location of certain qualities or things. Quick changes in the position of a bright light in the sky at night lead one to say that he has seen a "falling star." Throughout this movement, however, psy-chologically it is the same object that is doing the falling. Similarly in bodily changes, it is the same leg or arm or muscle that makes the movement, the perception being mediated by changes in spatial orientation of certain organic, kinaesthetic, and tactual qualities. In auditory movement, on the other hand, the situation is somewhat altered. In the playing of a scale, for example, the listener is unmistakably in the presence of psychological movement—but a movement of what? Is it the notes that are moving? If it is, then movement is taking place between different items, between qualities which lose their identity and change completely with each new note. To this extent the phenomenon is not the same as movement in visual and kinaesthetic fields. There it is the spatial location which varies and the qualities which are constant, while here the qualities are not constant, but are changing with each variation in pitch.

Furthermore, in the visual and kinaesthetic fields the movement is almost invariably that of a thing or object, whereas in music the movement is confined to sensory process changing its quality in time. The noises of everyday life do attach themselves to and become the signs of external objects, but the auditory materials of music very seldom shape themselves into forms which serve as symbols of objects. The sub-dominant triad does not represent a little boy sitting on a picket fence; nor does the movement set up by its resolution to the tonic triad mean that the boy fell off the fence. The movement in such a musical cadence comes as close to being *pure* movement as anything in the whole realm of phenomenological existence, and may therefore be regarded as an ideal movement in the sense that since it belongs to no particular things or objects, except the auditory qualities themselves, it represents, as it were, the essence of all movement. The reason for music's aloofness, its incorporeal and ethereal character, is in no small measure to be found in this fact of the relative absence of objective reference in tonal qualities. In no other art does the sensory material so greatly favor the aesthetic attitude of detached contemplation, so quickly remove the mind from its customary concern over the practical consequences of incoming impressions.

What the final explanation of auditory movement will be is still, of course, far from being known. The beginnings of an explanation, however, are to be found in the auditory qualities themselves. In the first section (pages 46*ff.*) it was suggested that the use of the words "high" and "low" for pitch need not be accounted for in terms of association by similarity. Phenomenologically high tones are actually perceived as occupying a higher spatial position than low tones. Since this is the case, the highness or lowness of a tone is an intrinsic property of the auditory quality itself. It is therefore no stranger that changes in auditory qualities which have different spatial signs should lead to the perception of movement than that similar changes in the visual and kinaesthetic fields should do likewise. At the level of perception, then, all movement is alike in at least one fundamental respect, namely, the change during an interval of time of the spatial position of sensory quality. The sensory qualities may be visual, auditory, or kinaesthetic, but their relation to certain spatial and temporal constants leads to the recognition of similarities in their forms of movement. What is strange, in the sense that it is still unexplained, is that there should be movement in any one of these three fields. In the present context, however, it is enough to point out that auditory movement, as well as visual and kinaesthetic, is an immediate fact of direct experience.

Thus it comes about that musical movement, which reaches the level of experience by way of an *objective* sense modality, contains properties and characters very similar to those found in bodily movement. So in spite of the fact that bodily movement is *subjective*, many of its forms and patterns find their counterpart in the objective domain of sound and tone. If a movement of the body is part of a subjective state which is appropriately described as indecisive and vacillating, musical phrases may also contain movements which possess the character of indecision and vacillation;

and the awareness of the latter does not depend or wait upon association by similarity or inference by analogy with the former.

13. *Music as the Language of Emotion*

The immediately preceding sections have prepared the way for the consideration of a view which not infrequently appears in modern as contrasted with older aesthetics, namely, the view or doctrine that art, and especially music, is the expression of emotion. Attempts to clarify this view have met, however, with two serious sources of confusion. In addition to committing the mistake of trying to make emotional quality the criterion of all art, writers who support this doctrine (1) either lose themselves in futile efforts to distinguish aesthetic emotions from real emotions or (2) fail to make it clear how an emotion, which is a subjective experience, can be expressed or embodied in a work of art, which is an objective event. The position defended in these sections circumvents both of these difficulties by insisting (1) that many so-called aesthetic emotions are, strictly speaking, not emotions at all, but are formal characters which have their locus within the objective processes of vision or audition, and (2) that, consequently, the problem of the embodiment of an emotion in a work of art need never arise for the simple reason that no emotion ever is embodied in a work of art. The *apparent* embodiment of emotion in a work of art is accounted for by the fact that visual and especially auditory processes intrinsically contain certain properties which, because of their close resemblance to certain characteristics in the subjective realm, are frequently confused with emotions proper.

The most recent thoroughgoing defense of the doctrine that art is the expression of emotion is to be found in the work of Ducasse.[68] Certain of his statements, however, leave the reader in doubt regarding the psychological mechanism by which feeling is objectified.

Form is important in aesthetic objects for the very reason that it itself, in contemplation, is the source of certain aesthetic *emotions* which nothing else can objectify . . . The feeling is apprehended as if it were a quality of the object. Nevertheless, when we are not actually going through the ecpathizing process, but describing it, we are well aware of the duality of object and subject, and of the fact that the feeling is experienced by the subject. From this descriptive standpoint, then, it is correct to say that *we* get the feeling out of the object.[69]

Now in spite of the fact that the position of the present book is closely akin to that maintained by

[68] C. J. Ducasse, *The Philosophy of Art*, 1929.
[69] *Ibid.*, 198, 177.

Ducasse, it must nevertheless be pointed out that Ducasse has unfortunately perpetuated one or two of the old confusions in aesthetics. Aesthetic emotion is regarded by him as a unique but puzzling species of real emotion, and what is still more unfortunate, the strength of his doctrine of objectified feeling is weakened by his admission that the objectivity is merely "as if"; that strictly the feeling is subjective and not, therefore, a property of the object. My own contention, on the contrary, is that if a work of art gives rise to emotion, the emotion is no different from any other kind of emotion; but that on account of their formal resemblance to certain subjective states, many truly objective properties are classified erroneously as emotions and included under the general head of aesthetic emotion.

So often have writers on the subject of music spoken of its intimate relation to feeling and emotion that it has now become a commonplace, even a platitude, to call music the language of emotion. If, as was stated above in another context, such a characterization is used carelessly or uncritically to mean the arousal and excitement of real emotions, then the aesthetician is entitled to go the whole length with Hanslick and deny that such emotions have anything to do with the proper nature of music itself, and also deplore the fact that music is thus lowered to the level of competing with those objects and events outside of art which succeed far better in stirring the emotions. But if it is the intention to suggest that emotional quality is an actual property of music itself, the means by which such a property may be revealed becomes a fundamental problem for psychological aesthetics. In spite of certain ambiguities of terminology, there can be no doubt that such is the intention of many writers who speak of the expression of emotion in music.

"Does not music stand for abstract qualities, for moods and emotions? Does it not represent the struggles and joys of the soul, if not the external realities of nature?"[70] Such has been the general tenor of persistent inquiries about the character of music. Although the author of these particular questions answers them emphatically in the negative, he nevertheless discloses a latent reservation that in some way emotion must be bound up with music when he asserts that "music is designed to appeal directly to something in us which is more primitive than thought and which is the source of thought—emotion. And we may rise to emotions as well as descend to them."[71]

[70] R. M. Eaton, "Music or Poetry," *The Musical Quarterly*, 1923, 9, 445*f.*
[71] *Ibid.*, 444.

The following excerpts from a recent writer on music leave no doubt as to the rôle assigned to music.

Mozart, developing the more homophonic idiom of Philip Emanuel Bach, brought to music a new emotional subjectivity, portraying the ebb and flow of moods with that ease and clarity which so completely reflects subjective emotional reactions . . . By breaking away from concrete and finite concepts, and by creating abstract forms from subjective impulses, music revealed that the subjective consciousness of man can express itself in an infinite variety of simultaneous motions and directions . . . Above all, it revealed that subjective experience can project itself into plastic forms as sound, and is best translatable through the auditory sense.[72]

"Could it be," asks another writer, "that the final object of musical expression is the endlessly intricate yet universal pattern of emotional life?"[73]

The expression of emotional life may not be the *final* object of music, if to be final means to be *decisive* or *single* to the exclusion of all other possibilities, but it is beyond doubt one very important and frequent aspect of tonal forms. It should perhaps be stated here once and for all, and with the greatest emphasis, that musical form can not, of course, *embody* or *contain* an emotion. Emotion is

[72] R. HARRIS, "The Crisis in Music," *The New Freeman*, 1930, I, 113.

[73] S. K. LANGER, *The Practice of Philosophy*, 1930, 161.

a matter of felt subjective experience and can not possibly reside in auditory structures. How, then, can music *present* or *express* emotional qualities? The answer to this question has already been formulated by implication in the preceding pages and is similar in many respects to the theory of logical form described by the author of the last question above. "Anything that can express something else has a similar structure. Just so far as the structures are similar, the expressiveness may go."[74] The structure or form of bodily process in emotion is shot through with movement. Countless introspective reports give evidence of this fact. The literal meaning of the word "emotion" implies the same fact—especially is this true of the corresponding German word for emotion, *Gemütsbewegung*, "movement of the mind." At the very onset of emotional behavior the muscles become tense and the entire body tends to contract. These movements, and subsequent movements of relaxation, have recently been accurately recorded by moving pictures.[75] They may be too fleeting for description by the person who has the emotion, but they undoubtedly contribute their share to the sense of change and movement which runs all through emo-

[74] *Ibid.*, 117.
[75] H. STRAUSS, "Das Zusammenschrecken," *Journal für Psychologie und Neurologie*, 1929, 39, 111–232.

tion. Not only, as a matter of fact, are the variations of underlying sensory process in emotion too elusive and fugitive for anything like accurate description, the nuances of the emotions and moods themselves are so numerous that words can not possibly be found to designate more than a few of them. And yet, as James said of the permutations and combinations of organic activities in emotion, so also of the profusion of motions in the kaleidoscopic patterns of tonal structure: it is abstractly possible that no shade of emotion, however slight, should be without a reverberating musical form as unique, even if it never finds a name, as the subjective state itself. Failure to fix the character of a musical form by a specific word is no sign that the character does not exist. Who can find words to describe the mood which runs through the first movement of Mozart's great G-minor string quintet? But who will declare, for that reason, that the mood is not there?

The similarity between tonal forms and kinaesthetic-organic forms, and the use of the same words to describe both, have been the source of much confusion in psychological theories of music. It is questionable whether any but the most critical readers of these pages will come free of this confusion. For the practical musician, of course, the confusion is of no great moment. What difference does it make to him whether the emotional character of music is thought of as a subjective commotion in the listener or as an objective property of music itself? For the theoretical psychologist or aesthetician, however, it is most certainly not a matter of indifference which of these alternatives is adopted. How far on the right road would theory get if the explanation for a given phenomenon started with kinaesthetic sensation when the phenomenon in question belonged actually in the auditory field? A recent very excellent experimental study of the effects of music shows, at one point, the difficulties created by not considering the possibility that the emotions "accompanying" the music or "suggested by" the music were in all strictness qualities inherent in the music itself.[76]

The listeners were told to make note of any emotions or moods suggested by the compositions. These emotional states were referred to as playful, whimsical, triumphant, powerful, martial, majestic, calm, peaceful, hurrying, restless, struggling, bewildering, tumultuous, uncertain, suspense, *etc.* Most of these words, when used for subjective moods, stand for psychological experiences which

[76] M. F. WASHBURN and G. L. DICKINSON, "The Sources and Nature of the Affective Reaction to Instrumental Music," in *The Effects of Music*, 1927, edited by Max Schoen, 121–130.

include among their components various forms of movement. In so far as similar forms of movement may be presented tonally, the same words apply equally well to musical effects. A person says, for example, that he feels restless. A description of what it feels like to be restless might include references to such things as increased rate of breathing and heartbeat, unsteady organics in the region of the diaphragm, tapping of the feet or fingers, inability to keep still, *etc*. It requires no great knowledge of music to appreciate the fact that much the same kind of movements may easily be produced in musical phrases. Staccato passages, trills, strong accents, quavers, rapid accelerandos and crescendos, shakes, wide jumps in pitch—all such devices conduce to the creation of an auditory structure which is appropriately described as restless. The passages for strings which interrupt the first development of the Meistersinger theme in Wagner's Prelude to *Die Meistersinger von Nürnberg*, or the marcato measures which follow the duet for violas and cellos in the first movement of Brahms' Second Symphony may serve as examples. If a person is asked to note any mood which occurs while he is listening to music, he may use the word "restless" without making it clear whether he meant that he himself felt restless or that the music itself possessed the character of restlessness.

In the experiment of Washburn and Dickinson no effort was made to preclude such equivocality. Many of the observers, in following uncritically the instructions to report accompanying moods, may have been describing the true character of the music and not the way they themselves felt. The reports were all included, however, under the head of emotion, which presumably meant felt subjective emotion. An interesting dilemma therefore faced the authors in their conclusions. Many of the moods reported would have to be classified under the unpleasant emotional states, and yet the observers all enjoyed the music! "Since all of the comments which have thus been classified were accompanied by judgments ascribing some degree of pleasantness to the compositions that inspired them, it is clear that none of the unpleasant emotions indicated could have exceeded the mild unpleasantness which is compatible with aesthetic enjoyment."[77]

How far can unpleasantness go before it is incompatible with aesthetic enjoyment? Can a person *enjoy* music and have an *unpleasant* emotion at the same time? Are there mixed feelings? Such troublesome questions as these must be answered if it is assumed that a person's pleasure in a work of art can be accompanied by displeasure, but they need never be raised if it is discovered that the

[77] *Ibid.*, 129.

so-called emotions are really not emotions at all, but are characters of the music which bear a striking formal resemblance to emotion. In the fugue from the funeral march in Beethoven's *Eroica* the fortissimo clashing of the dissonances and the pounding of the double against the triple rhythms build up for some twelve or fifteen relentless measures the inescapable impression of bitter strife and acute anguish. Now bitter strife and anguish, if felt as one's own emotions, are intensely unpleasant. But is the listening to the second movement of Beethoven's Third Symphony an intensely unpleasant experience?

In view of such facts as these, aestheticians have pondered much over the unreality or illusory quality of *aesthetic* emotions—as if there would not be something unreal and illusory about an emotion which is not an emotion at all! Or they have subscribed to some such view as Ruskin's, namely, that to describe objective experience in terms of subjective qualities is a pathetic fallacy. Both of these views lead to dubious theory, in spite of the element of truth which they contain. If a work of art stirs a real emotion, then it is legitimate enough to call it an aesthetic emotion simply because it was present during an aesthetic experience. It is questionable, however, whether such an emotion differs from emotion in general. According to this procedure one might go on indefinitely speaking of economic, theological, military, social, domestic, academic, political, patriotic, scientific, and many other kinds of emotion. As for the pathetic fallacy, it is true, of course, that in many cases subjective qualities are erroneously ascribed to objects. But it is also true that many objects, especially the numberless forms of tonal movement, possess characters which because of their close likeness to those found in the subjective realm are perfectly accurately described by words taken from subjective experiences.

Who knows, as a matter of fact, whether words used for subjective moods were originally applied to subjective or to objective states? Was the word "agitated," e.g., first used to describe the way a person felt, or to describe the appearance of ocean-waves in a storm and the sound of winds rushing through trees? Let the philologists come to the aid of psychologists in this matter. It is an interesting and, for the present context, a very pertinent fact that the word "emotion" itself was first used in English for objective events. Its very first usage was literal, in the sense of moving out or about. "The divers emotions of the Turkes." "Some accidental emotion of the center of gravity."[78] It

[78] R. Knolles, *The Generall Historie of the Turkes*, 1621, 3. J. Woodward, *An Essay Towards a Natural History of the Earth*, 1723, 45.

then acquired the meaning of any general disturbance or perturbation *in external events*. "Soon after, we had two or three of the greatest Flashes of Lightning, and the Noise of Thunder that succeeded them was so very great, and caused so great an Emotion in the Air, that it made the Rooms shake."[79] "And the waters continuing in the caverns, up to the very place of the hole, began to produce that dull noise, caused the emotion or earthquake, and finished with the violent wind forced up thro' the hole; after which the water returned into the sea, and having no further impelling cause, on account of the waves, rendered everything quiet again."[80] Which is the pathetic fallacy, the use of the word "emotion" for external movements and turbulence, or its application to subjective mental states? The cryptical answer, neither and both, is manifestly the only correct one.

Is music, then, the language of emotion? It all depends upon what one means by emotion. It is *not*

[79] "Part of a letter from Orlando Bridgman, Esq.; F.R.S. to Capt. Wine, giving an Account of a Storm of Thunder and Lightning that happen'd at Ipswich, July 16, 1708," *Philosophical Transactions of the Royal Society of London*, 1708, 26, 138.

[80] J. A. PEYSSONEL, "Observations upon a slight Earthquake, tho' very particular, which may lead to the Knowledge of the Cause of great and violent ones, that ravage whole Countries, and overturn Cities," *ibid.*, 1758, 50, 647.

the language of emotion if that phrase is taken to mean that a given composition is capable of arousing a subjective feeling on the part of the listener. It may, or it may not do this, and whether it does or not is irrelevant to the character of music itself. If, on the other hand, the phrase is intended to refer to an intrinsic character of music's moving tonal architecture, one must then most certainly recognize in it, however bad and ambiguous the wording may be, an attempt to single out a property of auditory form which gives to music a richness and power not exceeded, if in fact it is equalled, by any other art.

It is perhaps unfortunate, for a theoretical understanding of music, that these characters of tonal movement, because of their formal affinity to bodily movements, are so frequently described by words which also denote moods and emotions, for these auditory characters are not emotions at all. They merely *sound* the way moods *feel*. Hence the ambiguity of the phrase "language of the emotions." More often than not these formal characters of music go unnamed: they are simply what the music is, and by their presence, whether named or not, they give to any composition its distinctive style. Bach's G-minor Fugue for organ is very different in character from Wagner's Prelude to *Tristan und Isolde*. And this difference is more than the difference in notes, rhythms, accents, and harmonies employed. These latter items only serve to account for some of the conditions that make the difference. They are not themselves the differentiating character. The fugue is rigid, majestic, unrelenting in its onward sweep, possessed of tremendous energy—words are feeble instruments to describe its character. *Solvitur audiendo.* The Prelude is ardent, erotic, full of suspense, longing, unfulfillment. It is this individualizing quality of a musical composition, usually so far beyond the reach of words, that the phrase "character of musical form" is intended to comprehend. Language of the emotions—yes; but emotions removed from the sphere of bodily sensation and presented to the listening ear through the sensuous medium of moving, meaningless, wondrous sounds.

Part III

The Meaning of Music

1. *Autonomous Music*

Most of the problems which have been raised in the aesthetics of music turn out to be ramifications of a single persistent theme. Is the subject-matter of music to be accounted for solely in terms of the tonal structure itself, or is it necessary, for a complete account of music, to recognize the existence of a subject which, although symbolized by the music, is itself beyond the limits of tonal form and material?

Whenever it is maintained that the nature or essence of music lies wholly within the borders of sound and tone, that music is *sui generis* and never serves as a sign, an expression, a symbol, an imitation, a language, or a likeness of anything except itself, when, in other words, it is held that the laws of music derive solely from the laws of hearing, then music is considered to be *autonomous*. Many aestheticians, however, and even musicians, feel a certain incompleteness in any doctrine which defines music as autonomous. Is not the content of music more than the music itself? Does not music furnish to the listener an incarnation or representation of a world not made by sounds alone, a world of ideas and values communicated by way of music, but not identical with it? Whenever these questions receive an affirmative answer, music is regarded as *heteronomous*.[1]

All of the characteristics of music dealt with in Parts I and II of the present volume have been interpreted as autonomous. Surely no objections can be raised to such an interpretation when applied to the materials of music. The sheer tonal quality of music is simply just tone, and nothing but tone in all of its attributive aspects. Neither should any serious doubt be felt towards the possibility of extending the same interpretation to tonal form, to the innumerable patterns of moving sound moulded by the talent or genius of the composer. Tonal form *may*, to be sure, acquire reference to something non-tonal, but the perception of form *qua* form does not depend for its existence upon supplementation by properties not inherent in the form itself. The properties of musical form may

[1] A systematic and detailed survey of the many and varied doctrines which have been advanced in support of these two opposing views may be found in F. M. GATZ, *Musik-Aesthetik in ihren Hauptrichtungen*, 1929.

therefore be looked upon also as autonomous, a position accepted by the so-called formalists in musical theory and best presented by the famous anti-Wagnerian critic Hanslick. It was the chief purpose of the concluding sections of Part II, however, to suggest that the formalists have generally forced musical form into altogether too narrow confines, thereby handing over to heteronomy (or meaning) many valuable musical effects which do not rightfully belong there.

Every moving form of music has an intrinsic and individualizing character, the word for which, if happily one is found, more often than not applies equally well to the bodily qualities of mood and emotion. In order to demonstrate that these characters of musical form are tonally autonomous, and not erroneously "read into" the music out of the subjective experience of the listener, it would have to be shown that they are functionally related to certain aspects of the stimulus (the criterion for form adopted in Part I) or, in case the lack of suitable technique makes the discovery of this relationship very difficult, that any given character is judged by different people as belonging to the same musical structure.

In the absence of extensive experimental proof, the validity of the conviction that the character of musical form is autonomous must still rest more upon indirect than upon direct evidence. Real emotion is saturated with kinaesthetic and organic forms of movement. If movement were confined exclusively to these fields, then it would be idle ever to raise the question of the character of non-bodily movement, for the simple reason that no such movement could possibly be discovered. Since, however, movement is fully as characteristic of visual and auditory sensation as it is of somatic sensation, the conclusion is natural enough that the character which presents itself in one must also reveal itself in the other, so that if bodily states give the feeling of suspense, calm, restlessness, or finality, the moving patterns of auditory process may very fittingly be described in similar terms.

Laboratory evidence of the relation of musical character to aspects of the sound-stimulus is not, however, wholly lacking. One example will be sufficient to indicate the type of relationship. Certain musical phrases as they approach the last note give a sense of finality, others do not. Is this character of finality one which is "read into" the phrase by some process of association or supplementation, or is it intrinsic to the tonal form itself? In accordance with the definition of form previously given, the character is tonally autonomous if it depends upon certain aspects of the stimulus. Considerable experimental material is at hand which leaves no doubt that finality is inherent in certain auditory sequences, and not in others.[2]

Finality is a function of four stimulus-variables: power of two, simplicity of ratio, falling inflection, and width of interval. If three of these factors are kept constant and the fourth varied, a generalization can always be stated in terms of each of the variables to the effect that of two sequences of tones the more *final* one is that in which (1) the power of two occurs on the last note, (2) the last two notes sustain the simpler ratio, (3) the order of vibration-frequencies is from greater to smaller, and (4) the difference between the frequencies of the last two notes is smaller. In any one phrase more than one variable, of course, is at work. The more difficult problem is then to determine the *relative* influence of the four variables. In spite of troublesome complications this task has been accomplished by means of certain methods of mathematical weighting. For the present purposes it is enough to point out that ways may be devised for analysing out the relation of musical character to stimulus-conditions.

[2] The most elaborate treatment of the stimulus-conditions for finality is to be found in an unpublished thesis by K. E. Zener in the Harvard University Library. A less complete survey may be found in W. V. BINGHAM, "Studies in Melody," *Psychological Review Monographs*, 1910, No. 50.

Further justification for regarding musical character as autonomous comes from the fact that a given musical composition tends to be described in much the same way by different people. If the character thus described were a matter of association, meaning, suggestion, inference, or what not; if, in short, it were heteronomous and not autonomous, different individuals would not agree among themselves, for meanings are too individualistic. If you were asked to give the meaning of a verbal sound spelled either R-o-m-e or r-o-a-m, you might think of a city among the hills, Virgil, the capital of Italy, the Pope, wandering through the fields, *etc.*, *etc.* There would be no constancy between the meaning and the sound of the word. If the sound itself, however, or rather, the impression created by a series of sounds is much the same for a number of people, one is more entitled to suppose that this impression is intrinsic to the auditory material.

Whenever people are asked to state what a composition *means* (provided they are willing to admit that it has any meaning at all), disagreement is rife. Many careful studies and countless casual observations lend abundant support to this fact. What is often overlooked in these observations, however, is that although the meaning of a composition usually varies from individual to individual, the character, mood, emotional quality, or whatever word is used to indicate the general effect of the music, remains surprisingly constant and uniform. A striking illustration of the variability of meaning as contrasted with the uniformity of character revealed by music was reported at some length a number of years ago.[3] Some thirty musicians were asked to report their impressions of different compositions directly after they had been played. For some selections they were asked to note any ideas or meanings conveyed by the music; for others they were requested to describe the mood or character of the music. The complete disagreement of the reports under the first instruction was little short of ludicrous, whereas one can hardly fail to be very much impressed by the similarity of judgment given under the second instruction. The *Andante molto contabile* from Beethoven's piano Sonata in E, *Op.* 109, to cite only one example, came under the instruction to describe the general mood or atmosphere of the music. Such words and phrases as peaceful, pensive, subdued happiness, serene, placid, calm dignity, and tender happiness occurred frequently, and not a single description was given which could be considered as representing more than a slight divergence from the element

[3] B. I. GILMAN, "Report on an Experimental Test of Musical Expressiveness," *American Journal of Psychology*, 1892, 4, 558–576.

which these words undoubtedly share in common. In view of the difficulty which anyone would have in trying to put into words the purely musical quality of a composition, one is surely justified in supposing that the use of words so much alike indicates the presence in the music of a character determined not by extraneous associations, but by intrinsic properties of the music itself.

2. *Heteronomous Music*

The fact must nevertheless be recognized that for many people music carries an extraneous meaning, using the word "meaning" for those qualities which reveal no correspondence with the physical aspects of the stimulus, or, what amounts to the same thing, those qualities which have been acquired by an object through association and suggestion. For such people music stands for something other than itself, it possesses a subject or content which is non-tonal. Such musical experiences are heteronomous.

In the feverish debates by critics and musicians over the meaning of music, it is often far from clear just what the issue is supposed to be. With respect to form, and autonomous music in general, the question as to what it is like in any given piece of music differs markedly from the parallel question regarding meaning. It is legitimate, for the sake of convenience, to speak of form *as though* it were independent of the listener, although actually, of course, form can not exist unless someone is present to perceive it. But since the conditions for form reside partially within the stimulus, it is always correct to regard form as a potential property of musical experience, so that if a person fails to perceive a given form it becomes sound educational practice, unless the person is hopelessly insensitive or apathetic to music, to direct and guide his habits of listening until he does perceive it. This fact alone is sufficient justification for the wise musician's insistence that music, and nothing but music, should be the goal of instruction in appreciation. The situation is analogous to that of the overtones of the oboe discussed in Part I. Overtones only exist when someone hears them, but since they depend upon certain stateable aspects of the stimulus it is correct to assume that any person with a reasonably good ear will hear them if he has his attention directed to them. As much can not be said of meaning.

Meaning is the product of supplementary associations and suggestions, and is therefore not correlated with the stimulus-conditions that underlie the particular experience which serves as a symbol for the supplementary qualities. From this it must follow that nothing in the bare material and form of a given experience is able to command a specific meaning. A given musical experience may be accepted as incomparably wonderful in its own right. It may afford the listener the most exquisite satisfaction and pleasure. But whether it has a meaning or not depends upon the listener, not upon the music. The musician is therefore right when he insists that no musical form can give rise to the same meaning in different listeners. He is also correct when he argues with enthusiasm that for many lovers of music no meanings whatever are present in their enjoyment of tonal forms. He is definitely wrong, however, if he maintains that music can not have a meaning. For many listeners music is heteronomous, and no amount of pleading that it ought not to be can alter the fact that it is.

Since the heteronomy of music is always a matter of individual supplementation, there can be no point, as far as aesthetic theory is concerned, in trying to discover the variety of meanings which can be added to the sensory form of musical experience. It is of interest, however, to inquire whether through the welter of meanings which it must be granted may develop in the minds of some people when listening to music, there runs a central current of suggestion stronger and more direct than the countless eddies. Is it possible that the general character of musical form is such as to lead more smoothly and imperceptibly to one kind of non-tonal reverie and vision than to any other? Since many great writers on the subject of music have firmly believed tonal architecture capable of pointing to definite heights beyond the region of pure sound, it will be the burden of these closing sections to examine briefly the most famous and significant theory of the meaning of music.

3. Schopenhauer's Theory

Music stands alone, quite cut off from all the other arts In it we do not recognize the copy or repetition of any Idea of existence in the world. Yet it is such a great and exceedingly noble art, its effect on the inmost nature of man is so powerful, and it is so entirely and deeply understood by him in his inmost consciousness as a perfectly universal language, the distinctness of which surpasses even that of the perceptible world itself, that we certainly have more to look for in it than an *exercitum arithmeticae occultum nescientis se numerare animi*, which Leibnitz called it . . . Yet he was perfectly right, as he considered only its immediate external significance, its form. But if it were nothing more, the satisfaction which it affords would be like that which we feel when a sum in arithmetic comes out right, and could not be that intense pleasure with which we see the deepest recesses of our nature find utterance . . . The (Platonic) Ideas are the adequate objectification of will. To excite or suggest the knowledge of these by means of the representation of particular things (for works of art themselves are always representations of particular things) is the end of all the other arts, which can only be attained by a corresponding change in the knowing subject. Thus all these arts objectify the will indirectly only by means of the Ideas . . . Music is as *direct* an objectification and copy of the whole *will* as the world itself, nay, even as the Ideas, whose multiplied manifestation constitutes the world of individual things. Music is thus by no means like the other arts, the copy of the Ideas, but the *copy of the will itself*, whose objectivity the Ideas are. This is why the effect of music is so much more powerful and penetrating than that of the other arts, for they speak only of shadows, but it speaks of the thing itself.[4]

In these words, written over one hundred years ago, we find the substance of Schopenhauer's attempt to account for what he considered the unique power and meaning of music. Towards the end of the third book of *Die Welt als Wille und Vorstellung* he treats of the several arts and argues that they are the means by which the man of genius, he who has learned to view things independent of the principle of sufficient reason, embodies and communicates his knowledge of that which is essential and abiding in the phenomena of the world. To music, however, Schopenhauer assigns a unique place among the arts. Whereas the other arts give revelations of the eternal Ideas, of which our phenomenal world

[4] A. SCHOPENHAUER, *The World as Will and Idea*, trans. 1883 by R. B. Haldane and J. Kemp, Vol. I, 330 *f.*

is merely a manifestation, music deals neither with Ideas, which are the direct and adequate objectivity of the will, nor with any of their modes of appearance. Music is a direct expression of the will itself, not by way of the usual objects of perception, for these are only the reflections of the will in palpable form in accordance with the principle of sufficient reason, but by effective embodiment of the inner nature of all phenomena, their striving, longing, sorrow, joy, pain, merriment, or peace of mind.

The high place accorded to music was naturally a source of gratification to those few musicians who gave themselves concern for matters of theory or criticism. Wagner, in particular, was greatly impressed by the writings of Schopenhauer and was especially astonished by the philosopher's noble conception of music. He tells us that for many years he kept *Die Welt als Wille und Vorstellung* always near at hand and that during the first of these years he studied the whole of it four times. It is not difficult to believe him when he insists that if "in later years I again expressed opinions in my casual writings on matters pertaining to that art which so particularly interested me, it is certain that traces of what I learned from my study of Schopenhauer's philosophy were clearly perceptible," though credulity is strained a bit by his later assertion that it was some such serious mood as that created by the study of Schopenhauer which inspired the conception of *Tristan und Isolde*.[5] Schopenhauer's influence, however, among those who practice the art of music has been, naturally enough, very sporadic, though hardly less so than that of any other writer on the aesthetics of tonal art. The finest products of musical genius are rarely accompanied by scholarly application to the problems of aesthetic theory. It is very possibly, for that reason, none too auspicious a sign that so many musicians of today are keenly alive to the various theoretical interpretations of their art. But the views of these younger intellectual musicians, if put in systematic form, would hardly correspond to the heteronomous theories of writers like Hegel, Schelling, Oersted, and Schopenhauer. They would resemble more closely the autonomous doctrines of Hanslick.

Even the philosophers themselves have not taken Schopenhauer's views on music too seriously. There is an element of the fantastic, even of the impossible, in his speculation, which weakens the conviction carried by the whole. To argue that rise in pitch corresponds to ascending grades in adequate objectifications of will, that departure from pure intervals caused by equal temperament is analogous to the deviation of the individual from the type of

[5] R. WAGNER, *My Life*, trans. 1911, Vol. II, 616f.

the species, or that in a melody of the treble there may be recognised the intellectual life and effort of man is to invite ridicule even from philosophers unacquainted with musical technique. It is, moreover, difficult to avoid the suspicion that Schopenhauer found his theory of music congenial not so much because of its intrinsic ability to explain the richness of musical experience as because of the neatness with which it complemented his theory of art in general and his system of philosophy as a whole.

Sculpture, painting, poetry: these arts obviously make use of materials which may be comprehended within that portion of a philosophical system treating of ideas and objects of thoughts. But music presents an enigma, for its tonal patterns trace no objects of thought, no ideas of the phenomenal world. And yet it seems possessed of a universal language and a profoundly emotional appeal. The other arts move within a world of phenomena, within the shadows of reality. What more effective way of meeting the problem of music than by setting it apart from all shadows and phenomena and assigning it a place within the in-itself of all appearances?

Yet in spite of the infirmities which one may discover in Schopenhauer's theory of music there nevertheless exists at the heart of it a vitality which defies the action of ridicule and neglect. Not least among its virtues is the unique place in aesthetic theory which it has secured for music, and the striking and forceful manner in which it has sensitized philosophers and musicians to the problem of music's ineffable and mysterious charm. The elaboration of the theory is hardly less elusive than the musical effects which it purports to elucidate. Yet if one is prone to believe that "exact" aestheticians like Fechner and Stumpf have thus far missed the kernel of musical experience, that even the formalists interpret that experience too narrowly, it is then possible to believe that nowhere in aesthetic theory can one bring to light a happier insight into the nature of musical meaning and the basis of its peculiar magic than the one suggested by Schopenhauer. But the theory, in order to do justice to the facts of musical experience, must be expanded and freed of its mystical element. As put forth by its author it seems too much the product of sheer intuition—using the word intuition in the sense of a judgment which has few, if any, conscious connections with items which could offer logical support for the conclusion contained within the judgment. Schopenhauer concludes that music is a direct copy of the will itself. Are there any psychological items which might compel assent to such a bare conclusion?

4. *Dynamism*

Interpenetrating the purely auditory core of
every musical experience, whether it be a single
tone or a Wagnerian orchestral cloudburst, there
may be found a trace of psychological material
from the somatic senses. These materials range in
complexity from the simplest sort of tactile component involved in the perception of single tones
to the enormously intricate network of sensory
and imaginal organics and kinaesthetics set into
operation by full musical scores, and may, for the
sake of convenience, all be included under the term
"dynamism," signifying thereby the active, personal, mobile character which seems to attach to
most bodily sensations. A consideration of these
somatic additions to the auditory groundwork of
the musical consciousness will seem to rob music
of its elegance and purity, or, at best, to leave it
at the prosaic level of a chapter on visceral sensations. Such is the fate of a good deal of psychological analysis. The intimate warmth and lively
activity of the original total experience vanish
when it is split up into logical aspects. But it is
only a pretty form of prejudice that makes us feel
that analysis of some given seraphic experience
into one sort of psychological material is more to
be desired than analysis into any other.

A hasty review of certain of the more relevant types of non-auditory factors in music, proceeding from the simple to the complex, will serve to clarify the notion of dynamism. Even in the perception of a simple tone there is not infrequently the admixture of a slight trace of tactile quality. Workers in the field of audition often have occasion to note, in the descriptions of supposedly pure auditory qualities, references to qualities which have a close approximation to those of touch. Low tones present very non-intensive puff-puffs and rumblings, middle tones a smooth purring, and high tones a soft hissing, which, although extremely difficult to disentangle from the auditory quality, are undoubtedly tactile in origin. With increase in intensity of the sounds the tactile component becomes unmistakable. The presence of such qualities in sound has a reasonable enough explanation. In some of the lower organisms, for example, fishes, the organs of the internal ear are intimately connected with cutaneous receptors of the same type. These structures form together a system of lateral line sense organs, and the nerves which supply the internal ear and the cutaneous organs terminate together in the acousticolateral area of the medulla oblongata. These structures, moreover, resemble very closely those found in the human internal ear. It is not at all unlikely that cutaneous organs, lateral line sense organs, and organs of the internal ear all developed phylogenetically from some more general type of tactile structure.

When, instead of listening to simple pure tones, one attends to the quality of clangs, *i.e.*, fundamentals with different sets and relative intensities of partials, there is little difficulty in recognising on the basis of their timbre the difference between tones of identical pitch and intensity. The distinguishing signs of different timbres are again undoubtedly due in some small measure to tactile qualities underlying auditory sensation. It is not mere analogy or figure of speech which leads us to call a French horn smooth, a piccolo sharp, an oboe astringent, the voices of some singers silken, a violoncello velvety, and a bassoon or bass viol rough.

Much more striking are the effects of non-auditory qualities in tonal combinations, for here we are nearly always in the presence of beats of varying degrees of rapidity and intensity—beats which result from the juxtaposition of fundamentals, overtones, or difference-tones. The phenomenology of beats still needs further exploration, but it is probably safe to say that an appreciable portion of the total effect of beats is due to the intermixture of tactual material. Two tones which beat are often said, as a matter of fact, to pulsate. If anyone is in doubt about the tactile component in beats let him listen to the sounding of two strong diapason notes just a bit out of tune. When one remembers that the rapidity of beats equals the difference between the frequencies of the generators, and that the beating effect is altered with every slight change in either the absolute or relative intensities of the generators, and that even when there are only two tones present the generators which are adequate to the production of beats may, in certain cases, be two fundamentals, two overtones, two difference-tones, a fundamental and an overtone, a fundamental and a difference-tone and a difference-tone and overtone, he will be staggered to think of the well-nigh inexhaustible number of beating effects which must suffuse the tonal patterns of such scores as the Strauss tone-poems, where one hundred or more instruments weave their intricate structures of sixteen or twenty moving parts.

Why are these tactile processes not more obvious? There are various reasons. Many of the effects are subliminal. Even maximum attention to them would not reveal their presence. The beats from the partials of two soft tones would probably escape the keenest ear, although, even in such a case, it is not impossible that there is some very subtle difference in the total effect, even when it is extremely difficult to identify it as one of beats. Many other effects, easily perceptible when attention is directed to them, seldom enter the focus of musical attention. They form, as it were, a constantly shifting fringe or hazy periphery. But the chief reason why the somatic material of tone goes unnoticed is that under ordinary conditions of listening to music this somatic material is simply not there to be noticed. Tactual and kinaesthetic components of auditory sensation are gotten at only as the result of very careful observation. They are therefore to be regarded generally as artificial abstractions, not as real phenomenal entities residing within the auditory material. They play the rôle of physiological determinants, and are to be counted among the conditions which determine the quality of the auditory experience.[6]

Occasional effects are produced in music which even people untrained in this sort of analysis not infrequently speak of as possessing something not strictly tonal. When in a large orchestra thirty or forty strings are playing in unison it is humanly impossible for each of the players to produce a tone of exactly the right pitch, as a consequence of

[6] A very impressive survey of these effects of dynamism as they appear in the works of different composers may be found in L. BOURGUÈS et A. DÉNERÉAZ, *La musique et la vie intérieure*, 1921.

which one hears a massed tone that, although it produces a psychologically single pitch, has about it something in the nature of a scintillating shimmer, a prickly sheen. The ear is being exposed to a sort of soft tickle, the quality of which is generally assigned immediately to the sound itself, although it has its origin closer to the cutaneous level. The same effect, in a more marked degree, may be heard on pipe organs which have *voix céleste* or *unda maris* stops. Here each tone comes from two pipes just enough out of tune with each other to produce two or three beats a second. When music of rich harmony is played on these stops the effect at times is indescribably lovely. There floats in and through and above and below the music a soft, illusive, sandpapery feeling which enhances in striking fashion the pleasing quality of the string-like tone of the pipes.

Persons who have become practiced in the description and analysis, under laboratory conditions, of the simple auditory materials which lie at the basis of musical experience find themselves obliged to draw upon words which apply to tactual and taste perceptions. In trying, for example, to characterize verbally some of the musical intervals, the octave is referred to as smooth, like the surface of window glass or polished steel; the fifth, as hollow and empty; the fourth, rough, like the feel of coarse sandpaper; the seventh, astringent, like the feel of small sharp granular objects; the sixth, luscious and succulent, like rich pudding-sauce; the third, mellow, like ripe fruit; and the second, gritty, like the feel of sand or small pebbles in the hand.[7] These strenuous efforts, absurd as they may sound to the musician who immediately identifies every interval without ever putting a qualitative name to it, to find words which will serve to characterize different tonal combinations reveal more than the mere poverty of language applicable to the world of sound: they point to the presence, among the conditions of tonal sensation, of factors which derive from the sense of touch. If it were possible to extend such characterizations to chords involving six or eight notes the need for borrowing descriptive terms from the domain of tactile experience would undoubtedly be felt even more keenly.

Up to this point we have considered chiefly what might be called the static or absolute values of dynamism, that is to say, those tactile qualities which attach to single tones or simple combinations of tones taken in isolation. Much more significant are the effects of dynamism which result

[7] E. M. EDMONDS and M. E. SMITH, "The Phenomenological Description of Musical Intervals," *American Journal of Psychology*, 1923, 34, 287–291.

from the use of tones in melody, harmony, and counterpoint, for here the static values are supplemented by a host of new ones which we may refer to as relative dynamism. Just as the quality of every note in a melody is partly determined by the notes which have gone before and partly by those which are going to follow (and the same for chords in harmonic progression), so the tactile factor is altered by its position in a sequence. If b is the tactile component of the note B, then, if B is used in the melody A, B, C, the quality of b becomes altered in such a sequence by virtue of its temporal relation to a and c. The vast number of new tactile qualities thus brought into play can be at least vaguely appreciated by bearing in mind the innumerable temporal patterns which the kaleidoscopic changes in musical melody and harmony can create.

These somatic factors, inasmuch as they underlie the dominant auditory components, presumably have a certain share in the *movement* of music. Whether, in complete isolation, they would be adequate to the appearance of tactile movement is difficult to say. But linked to mobile auditory qualities they must certainly partake to some extent of the variegated motions of their hosts, and must serve, moreover, to augment the vividness of tonal movement.

Further reinforcement of auditory movement is to be found in the kinaesthetic factors which accompany the production of tones by the human voice. In the beginning vocal kinaesthesis might well have served as a sort of measuring stick for the amount of qualitative separation between any pair of tones—for, consider the following fact: If one relaxes his vocal chords completely and sings in an effortless manner the note which quite naturally comes out of that position of the throat, he will discover, on repeated trials, that the pitch of the note thus produced is almost always exactly the same. There is, in other words, a tone of very definite and constant pitch which corresponds with a relaxed set of the vocal organs. Now, to produce a tone of some other pitch requires a certain readjustment of the vocal organs, a readjustment, moreover, which must be exactly the same each time if the new pitch is to be the same. If we call the first note A, and its corresponding kinaesthetic set, together with its local sign, a, and the second note B, and its kinaesthetic pattern b, then we may suppose that since A and a, and B and b are frequently linked together, and since between a and b, given in succession, a movement always takes place, this movement comes in time to accentuate the change from A to B. The mechanism would obviously not be so simple as its description sounds, but its principle can be surmised from the illustration.

The presence of kinaesthetic patterns of movement, the sort which may be looked upon as a form of vestigial vocal accompaniment, can be felt in certain striking musical passages. Ordinarily such effects are obscured, fortunately enough, by the listener's absorption in the tonal affective values of the composition. But by careful direction of attention they can be detected even by persons wholly unpracticed in the observation of sensory processes. If, in a rapid musical passage, like a glissando, the notes are close together in pitch the flow of sound is smooth and unbroken. Each muscular sensation, which would be brought into play if such a succession of notes were produced vocally, resolves itself into the next without let or hindrance, and the feel of the thing is easy and fluent, like the graceful gesture of a skilled dancer.

Passages like those which follow the announcement of the theme in the *Larghetto* of Mozart's clarinet quintet illustrate the point. Consider, on the other hand, the very different results secured by Chopin, for example, in the eleventh *Etude* of *Op.* 25, or the first *Scherzo*. Here the notes which are adjacent in time are anything but adjacent in pitch. In the rapid passages they fly about here, there, and everywhere, leaving between themselves wide tonal gaps filled in by swift darts of movement. In the *Etude* the semblance of chromatic continuity formed by the alternate notes is rudely broken into by wide jumps between the chromatic sequences. If such passages could be rendered vocally, the laryngeal musculature would be subjected to abrupt stresses and pulls caused by quick adjustments to sharp differences in spatial and intensive patterns, and the feel of the thing would be uneasy and jerky, less like the movements of a graceful dancer, more like those of a jumping jack. And it is not uncommon to hear musicians with no flair whatever for nice sensory distinctions speak of the strains and tensions, and even fatigue, which close listening to the swiftly moving parts of such compositions entails.

All musical movement, therefore, has about it something potentially kinaesthetic in character. The actualization of these kinaesthetic factors in the contextual form of movements of every kind and description and meaning depends to some extent on the ideational type of the listener, but more especially on such factors as pitch-differences between notes, tempo, intensity, timbre, and mode of emission of the primary auditory qualities. The preceding illustration singles out only one of the numerous ways in which kinaesthetic dynamism may operate. An enumeration of all the varieties of dynamism would be too tedious. One or two further illustrations must be sufficient.

Variations of tonal intensities (what the musicians call dynamics) may be applied to musical phrases in three different ways. There is an absolute intensity, the degree of loudness assigned to a phrase in its entirety; a relative intensity, secured by successive increments or decrements of loudness, the crescendos and diminuendos of music; and abrupt changes in the loudness of single notes either at regular or irregular intervals, which lead to the manifold varieties of musical rhythms and accents. Other things being equal, insistence and pervasiveness of tactile and kinaesthetic dynamism vary directly with the absolute amount of auditory intensity. And within the limits set by these absolute amounts the composer has at his disposal the possibility of innumerable variations in the mosaics of dynamism traced by the crescendos, diminuendos, rhythms, and accents of music.

One of the most remarkable effects of this sort is achieved by Wagner in the succession of crescendos and diminuendos during Isolde's passionate singing at the close of *Tristan und Isolde*. Nearly all the resources of dynamism are made use of, but the most telling one is undoubtedly that of the relative dynamics. The intensities of the whole array of instruments, as well as their general pitch-region, rise quickly to a climax (at first all within the compass of a single measure) on a chord which cries out in vain for a satisfactory harmonic resolution, and then fall back to the starting point, only to begin the crescendo all over again. This process continues, with gradual lengthening of the periods of rise and fall, through some sixteen measures, and culminates in a final and tremendous crescendo which entitles one to expect that the intensities will fall off in a burst of harmonies which satisfactorily resolve the chord of the climax. On the contrary, the chord, after two attempts, fails of resolution, a slow return to the tonic through ever-softening harmonies sets in, Isolde's voice trails off on a suspended fifth, and the curtain falls on the quietness which comes from physical exhaustion.

The intimate relationship between rhythm, accent, and kinaesthesis is too familiar to need elaboration. It is interesting to note, in passing, the greater emphasis being placed on rhythm by the moderns, some of whom affect a return to classicism by applying the forms of the fugue to rhythm rather than melodies. The practice may be merely a reaction to the romanticists' fondness for vague and indecisive rhythms, but it is more likely the result of a desire to find more adequate expression for the intensity and restlessness of modern life.

The tremendous bodily commotions stirred up by American jazz or a Strawinsky tone-poem are lost only on those who are blinded by their aversion to what they choose to consider the cheapness of the former and their disgust at the cacophony of the latter.

The effects of rhythm and accent are always set within the larger framework of tempo. Variations of time, as in the case of those of intensity, may be applied to musical phrases in three ways: the absolute values of the movement as a whole, the relative values of accelerandos and ritardandos, and the time-values assigned to individual notes for forming the endless variety of melodic temporal patterns. Other things being equal, dynamism increases with the speed of the tempi. The vast contrast between, let us say, the *Adoramus Te* of Palestrina and Ravel's *La Valse* is by no means to be accounted for solely in terms of tonal differences. These two works, as a matter of fact, furnish a striking illustration of the different use of dynamism in all its possible forms. In the *Poème chorégraphique* the strains of the wide pitch-gaps, the incessant tactile jarring of the dissonant intervals, the numerous $pp < ff$'s within a single short measure, the terrific crescendos by the combined forces of a roaring orchestra, and the final instruction to *pressez jusqu'à la fin*, these, and many other effects which must be heard and *felt* to be appreciated, lead to a bodily condition bordering on emotional collapse.

The music of Palestrina, on the other hand, belongs to an entirely different genus. Kinaesthetic dynamism is almost completely absent, and even the tactile qualities are reduced to a minimum (or were, at any rate, in the mind of the composer) by the selection of intervals belonging to pure intonation rather than to the tempered ratios of our present-day scales. Only twice in the upper voice of *Adoramus Te* are the adjacent notes of a phrase separated from each other by more than a whole tone, the tempo throughout is very slow and steady, the rise and fall of volume is gradual and restrained, and the occasional slight deviations from the normal accents of the long rhythm are ever so gently introduced and are much too subtle for comprehension by most jazz-Strawinsky-spoiled ears. By these means one is brought into the presence of a beauty and serenity which reside exclusively within the formal structure of tonal quality itself. Such music lacks the rich expressiveness achieved by later composers, but it possesses a loveliness of sheer tonal quality which only reappears, under a different form and style, in the eternal youthfulness of certain pages of Mozart.

The materials which enter into the formal structure of musical composition present an almost bewildering array of items. The pitches alone number well over a hundred. This number, when multiplied by the series of intensities and the various timbres of a large orchestra or pipe organ, mounts to fifty thousand or over on a conservative estimate. Tonal quality, moreover, quite apart from its combination into intervals and chords, has its own intrinsic pleasantness, especially as modified by different sets of overtones. The qualities of orchestral instruments and of human voices have their respective degrees of affective coloring. These items constitute the raw material of music. When, in the hands of a musical genius, they are moulded and shaped into the intervals and chords of harmony, accented and timed along the myriad paths of melody and counterpoint, caught up and carried along by the ceaseless change of auditory movement, and finally tempered by the nuances of dynamics and tempo—when, in short, they change from the *material* to the *form* of music, they present to the sensitive ear an unparalleled richness and complexity of tonal character which, although immediately perceptible and recognizable, is hopelessly indescribable in words.

In spite of the fact that the technique for the creation of good musical structure is exceedingly strict and involved, the form of music, paradoxically enough, is more plastic than that of any of the other arts. Its materials, in contrast to those of other arts, find no counterpart in nature. In the world about us we are constantly confronted with various sounds and noises, but seldom with periodic vibrations such as those selected for musical tones, and never with tones combined as they are by the art of the musician. This almost complete freedom and isolation from the world of everyday events is the priceless treasure of music, and one which enables the composer to give free rein to an imagination unhampered by any considerations of what Schopenhauer would call the principles of sufficient reason. Common sense, logic, morality, conformity or faithlessness to reality—these, thank God, have nothing to do with music.

5. *Musical Meanings Not Made of Sound*

If tonal quality were the sole material of musical structure, the position of the extreme formalists, like Hanslick, would be almost unassailable. Musical tones and their combinations are singularly unrepresentative of anything except themselves. Even tonal movement, inasmuch as it is the movement of meaningless auditory quality rather than the movement of a "thing," would presumably not

lead much beyond itself, were it not for the fact
that the dynamism of auditory sensation tends to
bridge the gap between the world of sound and the
world beyond.

Tonal movements which are set against a background of bodily processes fairly quiver with their
potential capacity for suggesting meanings both
near and remote. The sounds of music rise and
fall, soar and droop, leap and bound, surge and
tumble, quiver and flutter, throb and pulsate.
But so do our own bodies and the bodies of other
people, when giving expression to certain states of
mind, rise and fall, throb and pulsate. Hence it is
only a short step along the bridge which leads
away from sound and tone before one comes to
find in the ceaseless activity of music the aspira-
tion and longing, the striving and failure, the peace
and tenderness, and the strength and weakness of
his own active life. And it is only a bit farther in
this same direction that the beauty of pure music
tends to disappear as the conjurings of an everyday
imagination absorb and make concrete the illusive-
ness of tonal movement. Then it is that the realistic
mind, contaminated by program-notes and titles,
discovers the boy falling off the picket fence, the
locomotive climbing upgrade, and sees visions of
purple lilacs and deserted farms, a boyhood in
Mesopotamia, angels harping on their harps, Till

Eulenspiegel knocking over an apple-cart, and the wife hurling dishes at her noble spouse.

There is nothing in the wide world that a musical phrase can not mean when supplemented by associative bonds contributed by the listener or suggested by the composer or critic. If one is told that certain musical compositions represent the landing of the Pilgrims on Plymouth Rock or the political differences of the Democrats and Republicans, then, whenever these compositions are heard they will tend to carry the same meanings. These are obviously extreme cases of disjunction between the terms of a meaning-relationship. But they serve to illustrate the lengths to which people can and do go in their efforts to "interpret" what music is trying to convey. And I am not sure that the great mass of people who listen to music will not always saturate it with the free gifts of imaginations bounded by the horizon of a workaday world.

For those, however, who cling jealously to the loveliness of sheer tonal quality, the charm of the suggestions and meanings which hover close to the intrinsic character of music's formal structure lies chiefly in this, that these meanings just beyond the world of sound seldom reveal corporeal concreteness. The suggestion of personal struggle and effort, let us say, which music can so effectively convey, derives primarily from the close similarity between skillfully manipulated accents, rhythms, tempi, pitch-differences, and movement (plus the effects of dynamism), and the actions and motions of those who in real life struggle and strive, so that the perception of one not infrequently evokes the state of mind which was responsible for the other. Struggle in real life, however, involves real obstacles, thoughts of real things, palpable objects. Not so in music. The stuff of musical struggle can not, by itself alone, trace the dimensions of an object. It remains the essence of all struggle, divorced from real life and presented through a sensuous medium of wondrous beauty. It may, to be sure, become in the minds of some people the embodiment of a particular struggle—Daniel in the lions' den or Jonah in the whale—but these gratuitous interpretations are the surest evidence that the listener has wandered far from the beauty of music and the charm of intangible meaning.

And so it is with all the mental acts which music so readily suggests without bringing before the mind the contents which become the objects of these acts in real life. By its very nature music stands aloof from the phenomenal world in which we humans live and move and carry on our practical business, yet the personal quality of this living and moving is spread out before us through the power of musical heteronomy.

6. *The Will*

Since music never expresses the phenomenon, but only the inner nature, the will itself, Schopenhauer contended that "it does not therefore express this or that particular and definite joy, this or that sorrow, or pain, or horror, or delight, or merriment, or peace of mind; but joy, sorrow, pain, horror, delight, merriment, peace of mind *themselves*, to a certain extent in the abstract, their essential nature, without accessories, and therefore without their motives. Yet we completely understand them in this extracted quintessence."[8]

It is clear that Schopenhauer, in treating of music as a copy of the will itself, includes under the term "will" what modern psychology would call emotions or moods. Hence in considering his theory psychologically, it is well to remember that he really argues that music is a copy of the will *and* the emotions. The manner in which music of a purely autonomous nature presents qualities which, because of intimate formal resemblance to subjective bodily processes, often go by the name of emotion, has been treated at some length in the concluding sections of Part II. These tonal qualities possess the "essential nature" of emotions, "their extracted quintessence without accessories,

[8] A. Schopenhauer, *op. cit.*, 338.

and therefore without their motives." When the accessories and the motives enter the experience of the listener, music has then become heteronomous. Even in such music the nature of the emotional quality remains much the same for all listeners, only the accessories and motives have individualized themselves beyond the reach of anything in the music itself. One person will argue that a sorrowful piece of music is the requiem for a pet dog, another will insist that it portrays the pangs of unrequited love, while a third will be positive that it is a lament over the iniquities of Jerusalem. Critics will dispute over the question as to whether a Mozart quintet reflects the composer's grief over the death of his father, his irritation at the whims and caprice of Constanze, his worry over debts, or his remorse at the recollection of one of his particularly inopportune vulgarities. Who knows? Who cares—while listening to the music?

It is enough that for the searching there may be found in Mozart, along with the usual gayety and lightness of form, a hint now and then of wistful sadness and delicate melancholy which, for fineness of feeling and reserve of expression, are unmatched anywhere else in music. Here is sadness removed from the events to which it is bound in ordinary life. Here is Schopenhauer's abstracted quintessence of all sadness, the hearing of which affords to the listener a joy forever. Of such is the kingdom of music.

In suggesting that the most common element in musical heteronomy is the expression of will, it remains, in conclusion, merely to point out the relation between Schopenhauer's philosophical conception of the will and a more strictly psychological account of the will, and to inquire whether in the latter there may be found processes at work which will make the view of Schopenhauer more intelligible. As in the case of emotion, so with will, the introspective analysis given by James furnishes illuminating material. James says:

We may consequently set it down as certain, that *whether or no there be anything else in the mind at the moment when we consciously will a certain act, a mental conception made up of memory-images of these sensations, defining which special act it is, must be there . . . A supply of ideas of the various movements that are possible left in the memory by experiences of their involuntary performance is thus the first prerequisite of the voluntary life.*[9]

Although psychology since James has continued to stress the relevance to volition of kinaesthetic imagery of movement, it is not so true that at the present time will or volition would be

[9] W. JAMES, *Principles of Psychology*, 1890, Vol. II, 492, 488.

completely identified or made coextensive with ideas of movement. This difference of interpretation, however, would not alter the importance of these ideas of movement in volition. James continues:

My first thesis accordingly is that . . . *in perfectly simple voluntary acts there is nothing else in the mind but the kinaesthetic idea, thus defined, of what the act is to be . . . An anticipatory image, then, of the sensorial consequences of a movement, plus (on certain occasions) the fiat that these consequences shall become actual, is the only psychic state which introspection lets us discern as the forerunner of our voluntary acts.*[10]

Whatever else the will may be like psychologically, as contrasted with any philosophical conception of Will, one can hardly fail to recognize that ideas of action and movement are peculiarly germane to volitional consciousness. Now the burden of a goodly portion of the present volume has been that movement is an ever present datum in all music, whether autonomous or heteronomous. Owing to the manifold varieties of moving tonal forms which are immediately perceived in auditory structures, music tends, whenever it reaches beyond the realm of sound, to assume many of the characteristics which pertain to those movements with which everyone is most intimate and familiar,

[10] *Ibid.*, 492, 501.

namely, the movements of the human body which, in turn, must be of the same nature as those ideas of movement which serve as forerunners of voluntary action.

Thus does it come about that music, more nearly than any of the other arts, may be looked upon as *a copy of the will itself*, and that it seems to touch life so closely; for when one speaks of life in this vague sense he invariably means the decisions, struggles, actions, and efforts which adjustment to environment imposes upon every individual and which are generally thought of as exhibiting the operation of the will. "Music is certainly able," said Schopenhauer, "with the means at its disposal to express every movement of the will. Now the nature of man consists in this, that his will strives, is satisfied and strives anew, and so on forever." It is this human striving, in all its variety of manifestations, that music is able so poignantly to suggest.

Index of Names

Index of Subjects

A

B

C

D

E